C000069905

Contents

Introduction   2

Acts 4–8   8
Between Pentecost and Paul

Genesis 12–19   23
The long road of faith

John 8   38
Hard truths

Judges 2–16   49
The next generation

1 Corinthians 14–16   64
Messy but miraculous

Micah 1–7   72
The golden thread

John 9–12   81
A hero unlike any other

Ruth 1–4   96
Ordinary family, extraordinary future

Philippians 1–4   104
Joy amid opposition

SU article   4
Sport speaks of God

Spotlight on...   46
The Bible and me –
a writer's experience of the Bible

A golden thread

Through distant times a golden thread runs through our story. Over the next few weeks, as we read God's Word, we'll see it in the promise-filled life of Abraham, the not-so-good leaders of Judges, in Ruth's faithful commitment as a refugee, and in the prophet Micah's hopeful words, despite the hard truths of judgement.

In New Testament times the good news story continues in Paul's letter to the Corinthians – those 'miraculous but messy' times (Andy Bathgate). The golden thread runs through Paul's letter to the Philippians too, encouraging us to shine like stars. Supremely, we see and hear Jesus through the words of John's Gospel. He is Light in the darkness of our world and its story. It may be a long road, but Jesus walks with us.

As editors, we have some news to share with you. We're stepping down from our role in *Daily Bread* and are pleased to say that we're passing on this responsibility into the safe hands of **Sally Nash** from the next issue. This work has been a privilege and we're thankful to the team of writers who have brought God's light and encouragement to us over the past few years – and to the SU office team who bring it all to publication. We're thankful too to you, our readers, as together we walk this way and learn from God's Word.

As we were going to press we received the sad and shocking news that Andy Bathgate had passed away in his sleep. You will see that two of the last notes that he wrote were on 1 Corinthians 15! He wrote, 'Jesus has been raised, countering all that Adam spoiled. Adam's legacy is death. Jesus bequeaths life. He is raised and all those *in Christ* rise with him into new life and on the final day share Jesus' indestructible life.' We praise God for Andy's faithful life of service and encouragement to others. With him, we rejoice that: 'Death has been swallowed up in victory' (1 Corinthians 15:54).

'Tricia and Emlyn Williams
Editors

Daily Bread toolbox

'Tricia & Emlyn Williams worked with Scripture Union for many years. Emlyn led Schools ministry, then worked with SU International. 'Tricia was also part of the Schools team and later worked for SU Publishing, developing, writing and editing Bible resources. Having recently completed research in the area of faith and dementia, she continues with writing and editing faith resources. Retired from his role as discipleship pastor in a local church, Emlyn now continues his writing and talking ministries.

WAY IN

This page introduces both the notes and the writer. It sets the scene and tells you what you need to know to get into each series.

A DAY'S NOTE

The notes for each day include five key elements: *Prepare, Read* (the Bible passage for the day), *Explore, Respond* and *Bible in a year.* These are intended to provide a helpful way of meeting God in his Word.

PREPARE

Prepare yourself to meet with God and pray that the Holy Spirit will help you to understand and respond to what you read.

READ

Read the Bible passage, taking time to absorb and simply enjoy it. A verse or two from the Bible text is usually included on each page, but it's important to read the whole passage.

EXPLORE

Explore the meaning of the passage, listening for what God may be saying to you. Before you read the comment, ask yourself: what is the main point of this passage? What is God showing me about himself or about my life? Is there a promise or a command, a warning or example to take special notice of?

RESPOND

Respond to what God has shown you in the passage in worship and pray for yourself and others. Decide how to share your discoveries with others.

BIBLE IN A YEAR

If your aim is to know God and his Word more deeply, why not follow this plan and read the whole Bible in one year?

Sport speaks of God

Sport has huge appeal among young people and provides unique opportunities to connect with them, build relationships and share Jesus. Thanks to your support, we're able to help more churches than ever before to use this amazing medium for mission!

Scripture Union Sports Mission Team Leader Mark Oliver and his team – Sarah Bowey, Ruth Anderson and Holly Phipps – want every church in England and Wales to be able to make the most of the mission opportunities that sport can offer, whether that's just throwing a frisbee round the local park or running a sports-themed camp.

Mark says, 'We all have a responsibility to tell the next generation about Jesus. As we engage with children and young people, it's important that we do so in a way that is accessible to them. With more children and young people playing sport every Sunday than attending church, we know that sport speaks a language that they understand.'

A broad appeal to young people

Not every young person would consider themselves to be 'sporty' and Mark is keen to point out that in the context of mission, '... we're not just talking about competitive, conventional or organised sports such as football, netball or tennis. We include simple and fun physical games and activities too, things that appeal to most young people and require no previous experience to play.

'Mission through Sport brings the community together and helps young people from a variety of backgrounds to develop skills and confidence that are useful both on and off the pitch. It builds relationships and so provides a way in to sharing the good news about Jesus.'

Flexibility suits a range of church settings

Mission through sport can also be readily adapted to most contexts. Mark says, 'We've trained our Mission Enablers so that they can help Faith Guides run sports mission easily and effectively, whether they're from a big church with access to a playing field or a small rural church with more limited local facilities, or anything between.'

The team is also developing new off-the-shelf resources for churches to use. These are based on the Revealing Jesus mission framework. 'So, whether a church is connecting with young people for the first time, or helping them to explore faith, respond or grow spiritually, these Mission through Sport resources

will help,' explains Mark. 'For example, we've created a series of "Half-time talks" with videos and accompanying games which Faith Guides can use to share something from the Bible, linked to a games session. We're also developing an additional set of videos that the young people can access in their own time, which help them explore that week's theme in more depth.

'For those Faith Guides who want to go a step further and specialise in Mission through Sport, we're developing an accredited training course so they can construct their own programmes that are specifically tailored to the needs of the young people they work with.

'Mission through Sport is amazingly flexible – we really love showing churches how to make it a success in their particular circumstances!'

A missional game-changer

Having piloted lots of 'estate-based' sports programmes in the past few years, SU's Sports Mission Team is leading the way in supporting churches in low-income neighbourhoods to step out and reach the local children and young people.

Mark's passion is rooted in Isaiah 61 where we are instructed to 'bring good news to the poor'. He says, 'In such communities where I've worked, alongside the economic challenges, I've witnessed a poverty of hope. What greater hope is there than knowing Jesus? But a much higher proportion of churches in low-income communities have closed their doors than in affluent areas. We can use sports, games and fitness activities to make connections with children and young people and introduce them to Jesus. It can literally be a missional game-changer!

'It is such a privilege to work alongside churches and congregation members living and working on those estates. They are so willing to roll up their sleeves and get out into their communities and share God's love in practical ways.'

More intensive help

Getting Mission through Sport programmes off the ground in these areas is not always plain sailing and the churches involved often appreciate the extra practical help they can get from Mark and his team.

Holly Phipps is one of SU's two Sports Mission Pioneers and is based in Sheffield. She's been working with All Nations, a church founded on the Fir Vale estate in September 2022. In Easter 2023, Holly and Mark partnered with a team of church volunteers and Christians in Sport to run a three-day sports camp to connect with local young people. Over 30 came. They included Josh*, who arrived on the first day to see his friends who were at the event. Sadly, his attitude was disrespectful and his actions disruptive.

Mark says, 'My instinct was to send Josh home, but I felt that God had other plans. I decided to invite him back the next day on the condition that he got his parents to complete a consent form and that he changed his attitude. To my surprise, he returned.'

'I think I need Jesus to change me'

However, Josh's conduct was even more challenging on day two. 'He was resistant to everything we were doing to the point that his behaviour was spoiling things for everyone else,' recalls Mark. 'I spent time talking with him and could see that he had potential, but I didn't know how to get through to him.'

Nevertheless, Josh returned on the final day of the sports camp as Mark was preparing to share the good news of Jesus. 'It was one of the toughest groups I've ever had to face, but as I began speaking, the group went really quiet.

'At the end, I asked them to get into pairs and a member of the team went to speak with each pair. I found myself talking to Josh. He'd been really affected by the message I'd shared and what he said next was amazing: "I think I need Jesus to change me." And he meant it.

'Hearing that after the challenges of the previous days made it all worthwhile. Josh didn't become a Christian that day, but he did encounter hope and love on a sports field and now attends weekly sports sessions delivered by our team and the local church. God's love had started to dismantle the seemingly impenetrable wall of resistance that Josh had built around himself.

'Sport really can reach the hearts that other kinds of mission might not reach. My prayer is that many more churches will come to realise its value in sharing Jesus with a generation that don't yet know him.'

*Name changed to protect identity

A shorter version of this story first appeared in *Connecting You*, Scripture Union's free quarterly supporter magazine. If you'd like to receive copies of *Connecting You* and learn more of how God is moving in the hearts and lives of children and young people today, you can sign up on our website at su.org.uk/connectingyou.

Between Pentecost and Paul

This section of Acts is sometimes overlooked: the period between Pentecost and Paul. Yet it is a foundational time for the church. We see patterns established of daily gatherings, of sharing possessions and of preaching accompanied by miracles. We also see the beginnings of organisation and structure as deacons are appointed. In addition, this is the period of the first persecutions.

This series starts and ends with the first deaths within the early church. But what a contrast between them! Ananias and Sapphira forfeit their lives because they think they can lie to God. Stephen, on the other hand, is killed because he refuses to deny God. Together these deaths teach us that following Jesus is not to be taken lightly. We may face opposition for our faith, but that is surely better than facing the wrath of the Almighty God.

In these chapters we will meet ordinary Christians, some named but many not. Not many of us will be superstars of the faith like Peter and John or Paul, but in these early chapters of Acts we meet believers to whom we can all relate, from those who shared their wealth (4:34), to the unnamed voices bringing the widows to the apostles' attention (6:1), to those who buried Stephen (8:2) and those arrested by Saul (8:3). As we explore these texts, let's ask God to show us our own place in the story of the church.

About the writer
Alison Allen

After 14 years as a single missionary in Romania, Alison now lives in Suffolk with one husband, two children and three cats. She is currently in the final stages of a PhD in the Sociology of Religion, looking at British Millennials in international missions.

Giving freely

PREPARE
At the start of this week, bring to the Lord your plans, your hopes and your concerns.

· ·

READ
Acts 4:32 – 5:11

EXPLORE

This passage is unsettling to say the least! God takes the lives of an ordinary Christian couple because of a lie that was completely unnecessary. If they had simply said that they were keeping some money aside, nobody would have minded: the property was theirs to dispose of as they wished (5:4). But they chose to lie and paid for it with their lives. So why did they do it? It seems that Ananias and Sapphira were seeking prestige among the believers; perhaps they thought they could buy influence or position. Though the act of giving appeared generous, God saw through the facade. God cares more about the heart of the giver than the amount they give.

However, it is not only this story that I find unsettling. The first part of the passage also makes me uncomfortable. In a world where the accumulation of possessions is prized, sacrificial giving seems crazy. One could argue that it is better to steward resources well than to sell up and give the proceeds away. Barnabas could have paid people to farm his land, then given the food grown to the poor. The difference 2,000 years on is that we have lost the eternal perspective of the first believers: if you genuinely believe that Christ could return tomorrow, what use are more possessions (Luke 12:16–21)?

All the believers were one in heart and mind. No one claimed that any of their possessions was their own, but they shared everything they had.

Acts 4:32

RESPOND
Ask the Lord to show you what or how much he wants you to give, and to whom.

· ·

Bible in a year: 2 Chronicles 33,34; Psalms 75,76

Tuesday 2 July
Acts 5:12–16

Responses to the gospel

PREPARE
Do you need a miracle today? Ask God to intervene in your situation.

....

READ
Acts 5:12–16

EXPLORE
The early days of the church in Jerusalem must have been so exciting. People were being healed left, right and centre: even Peter's shadow was bringing healing. The apostles must have thought often of Jesus' promise that they would do greater works than he did (John 14:12).

Ignoring the first church was not an option for those living nearby: the believers gathered in a public place (v 12) and probably made a lot of noise. It's hard to keep quiet when you've just been miraculously healed! So the local people had to make a choice. Either believe and join the church (v 14) or keep as far away as possible (v 13). Indifference was not an option.

I wonder why people remained sceptical in the face of so many miracles. Maybe they thought it was all a fraud, or they might have believed the miracles to

be demonic, as Jesus was accused of in Matthew 12:24–28. Perhaps some foresaw the coming persecution and were afraid of what would happen to them if they joined. And maybe there were some who just wanted to get on with their ordinary lives and not have to face up to the fact that God was doing something new. I suspect many of the reasons are similar today.

Nevertheless, more and more men and women believed in the Lord and were added to their number.

Acts 5:14

RESPOND
Pray that God would make his presence known in your church community to such an extent that those on the outside respond to him.

....

Bible in a year: 2 Chronicles 35,36; Luke 1:39–80

The perils of preaching

PREPARE

Pray for brothers and sisters around the world who are imprisoned for sharing the gospel, that God would comfort them and fill them with boldness and wisdom.

READ

Acts 5:17–32

EXPLORE

The excitement of yesterday's passage quickly drew some unwelcome attention. The Sadducees (religious leaders) were jealous of the popularity of this new sect. Rather than recognising the hand of God in what was going on, they were worried that their position was being undermined.

It was not the first time that Peter and John had been arrested (Acts 4:3). At that time the religious leaders had not dared to punish them because of their popularity, but had nevertheless commanded them to stop preaching about Jesus (Acts 4:18). So where do they get their boldness to continue? First, they knew that their message was true (v 32). Secondly, an angel had just told them to keep preaching (v 20), reiterating the command of Jesus (Matthew 28:19).

I wonder if our own reticence to evangelise is because we sometimes lose sight of these two things. Maybe we don't really see Jesus' commands to share his message (Matthew 28:19) as aimed at ourselves. Or our fear of opposition or rejection may cloud our vision of the truth and urgency of the glorious gospel.

Peter and the other apostles replied: 'We must obey God rather than human beings!'

Acts 5:29

RESPOND

'Turn your eyes upon Jesus,/ Look full in his wonderful face,/ And the things of earth will grow strangely dim,/ In the light of his glory and grace' (Helen Howarth Lemmel, 1863–1961). Turn your eyes upon Jesus as you reflect on these lyrics.

Bible in a year: Ezra 1,2; Luke 2

Thursday 4 July
Acts 5:33–42

Fly on the wall

PREPARE
Ask the Lord to speak to you as you read his Word today.

. . . .

READ
Acts 5:33–42

EXPLORE
We saw yesterday that the religious leaders had imprisoned the apostles in an unsuccessful attempt to silence them. In today's passage, we are a fly on the wall listening in to their internal discussions as they try to work out what to do about this new group of fanatics. In yesterday's passage, the cause of their opposition to the apostles was jealousy (Acts 5:17). Today, though, they are angered by the apostles' theology (5:30–32) and refusal to acknowledge the Council's spiritual authority.

How do you react when you hear of spectacular church growth or revivals? If I am completely honest, my initial reaction can sometimes be jealousy or cynicism. I find myself having to examine my heart, rooting out that pharisaic pride that believes that God should bless me and my group or church rather than them. Gamaliel's advice in this passage is wise: watch from a distance and be slow to pass judgement (vs 38,39).

While we may not be in a position to order that the leaders of that successful movement be flogged (v 40), let's be careful not to use our words – whether in person or in online comments – to humiliate or undermine them in public. If later some do fall, let's be sorrowful rather than exultant.

'... if it is from God, you will not be able to stop these men; you will only find yourselves fighting against God.'

Acts 5:39

RESPOND
Pray for the leaders of a church or ministry that appears to be in a season of growth and blessing. Ask the Lord to help them remain faithful to the gospel.

. . . .

Bible in a year: Ezra 3,4; Luke 3

No favouritism

PREPARE

Meditate on the 'great multitude ... from every nation, tribe, people and language' that will worship together in heaven (Revelation 7:9).

READ

Acts 6:1–7

EXPLORE

The speed of the church's growth seems to have taken even the apostles by surprise. They kept preaching as they had from the start (5:42), but found that they were increasingly distracted by the practicalities of leading such a vast movement (v 1). As the church grew, food distribution was becoming less fair (v 1). People were becoming Christians from different backgrounds. The Hebraic Jews spoke Aramaic and may have been more theologically and ethically conservative than the Greek-speaking Hellenistic Jews. Already vulnerable because of their widowhood, these women were now overlooked because of prejudices and stereotypes.

We do not know much about the seven men chosen to take on the task of food distribution. Stephen and Philip we meet again later in Acts. There are various traditions attached to Procorus, Nicanor, Timon, Parmenas and Nicolas, but the only thing we know for sure is that Nicolas had converted to Judaism prior to becoming a Christian (v 5). This meant that the widows now had at least one advocate from their own background in a position of leadership. Prejudice has no place in the church, whether it is in the treatment of ordinary believers or in the appointment of leaders.

'... choose seven men from among you who are known to be full of the Spirit and wisdom.'

Acts 6:3

RESPOND

Ask the Lord to show you if you need to change in any way your attitudes or actions towards people of a different background.

Bible in a year: Ezra 5,6; Psalm 77

Whose opinion counts?

PREPARE
Sing a song of praise to God.

∙∙

READ
Acts 6:8–15

EXPLORE

There are two conflicting narratives in this passage: two different ways of seeing Stephen. On the one hand, there is the voice of Stephen's opponents (v 9) and those they influence (v 11). They are set on destroying Stephen's good reputation.

The second narrative is that of Luke, the writer of Acts. Having introduced us to Stephen in verse 5, Luke now tells us something of Stephen's ministry of miracles and healing (v 8). As opposition grows, Luke reminds us of Stephen's devotion to God (v 10). And as Stephen is brought before the religious council (the Sanhedrin), Luke tells us that his face is like an angel's (v 15). He is so steeped in God's presence that he glows! The mention of Moses in the previous verse serves as a reminder of another time when a servant of God had a face that shone (Exodus 34:29).

Have you ever felt as if your words or motives are misconstrued and misinterpreted to be used against you (vs 13,14)? It's unpleasant and you can feel helpless. People quickly jump on the bandwagon when criticism is being hurled at someone, without stopping to listen to what was actually said and done. Let's be those who care more about how God sees us than what people say.

> But they could not stand up against the wisdom the Spirit gave him as he spoke.
>
> **Acts 6:10**

RESPOND
Pray that you might be filled with 'the Spirit of wisdom and revelation' (Ephesians 1:17) in your interactions with those around you. Pray too for any high-profile Christians currently in the spotlight because of their views and beliefs.

∙∙

Bible in a year: Ezra 7,8; Luke 4

Feeling down?

PREPARE
What are you grateful for this week? Thank God for his faithfulness and goodness to you.

READ
Psalm 143

EXPLORE

David is in a hard place. The physical struggle (v 3) causes a spiritual struggle (v 4); his battle with a physical enemy leads to a battle with his emotions. Worse than the enemy's threats, though, is desperation for a sense of God's presence (vs 6,7). He's feeling hopeless. When circumstances get us down, it's easy to let our emotions spiral downwards too, losing sight of our ever-present God.

So what should we do when we're in a dark place? David actively reminds himself of the things God has done before (v 5), then lifts his hands in prayer (v 6) to that same God who is faithful (v 1) and whose love is unfailing (v 12). It's as if he's reaching up to a strong hand to pull him out of the pit.

There are two truths which David states at the start and end of this psalm. First, he remembers the righteousness of God. David cries out for help on the basis of God's righteousness and goodness rather than his own (v 2). Secondly, David refers to himself as God's servant. He knows he is in relationship with this faithful (v 1) and loving (v 12) God; his plea for help is not because of anything he has done but because he knows that he is loved.

I spread out my hands to you; I thirst for you like a parched land.

Psalm 143:6

RESPOND
Look again at verse 5. Take time to consider the things God has done: from creation to salvation, to the day you first encountered him.

Bible in a year: Ezra 9,10; Luke 5

Monday 8 July
Acts 7:1–16

The master plan

PREPARE
Thank God for the people he has used to teach you more about himself.

. . . .

READ
Acts 7:1–16

EXPLORE

I wonder if Stephen was even listening to the high priest's question (v 1)! His face was shining (6:15) and he was full of the Holy Spirit (6:10). I don't get the impression he was being like a politician and refusing to give a direct answer to a direct question. Rather, I suspect he was simply aware that everyone was watching him and waiting to hear what he would say, so he made full use of the opportunity to tell as many people as possible how the entire history of God's chosen people points to the coming of Jesus.

Stephen begins his retelling of Israel's history with Abraham, Isaac, Jacob and Joseph. His emphasis is on God's faithfulness and his nearness. God uses each of these lives to further his plans. Stephen must have carried the crowd with him as he recited the key events and God's promises.

One thing I'm sure didn't even cross Stephen's mind at this moment was the significance of his own role in God's great plan of salvation, which we will see in the coming days. We are called to walk in obedience to God day by day and moment by moment; we can never tell which of those acts of obedience will prove significant.

'... and afterwards they will come out of that country and worship me in this place.'

Acts 7:7

RESPOND
Thank the Lord for leading you in the past and ask him if there are any new ways in which he wants to use you in his master plan.

. . . .

Bible in a year: Nehemiah 1,2; Psalm 78:1–37

Called and chosen

PREPARE
Bring to the Lord any worries or fears that might distract you from his Word today.

. . . .

READ
Acts 7:17–34

EXPLORE
Stephen's retelling of the history of God's chosen people moves to their time of slavery in Egypt and the rise of Moses.

What stands out in Stephen's summary of the story is how God's hand is on Moses throughout. From the start he is 'no ordinary child' (v 20), then he becomes 'powerful in speech and action' (v 22). By the time he visits the enslaved Israelites, Moses appears to be aware that God has chosen him (v 25). The Israelites, however, are not ready to hear this, so Moses runs away. God remains with him and continues to bless him (v 29). Then we see his dramatic calling (vs 30–34) as God speaks to him through the burning bush.

Few of us will have a calling as dramatic as that of Moses! But God has a purpose for each one of us. Sometimes it might seem as if we've given up on his call or even that he has changed his mind:

Moses spent 40 years leading a quiet, unremarkable life (vs 29,30), but God had not forgotten him. Whether you are a child (v 20), in education (v 22), aged around 40 (v 23), at home with children (v 29) or aged 80 (v 30), God has not finished with you yet!

'I am the God of your fathers, the God of Abraham, Isaac and Jacob.'
Acts 7:32

RESPOND
Thank God that he does not give up on you even when you make mistakes. Tell him that you are still available to be used in his plans (if you dare!).

. . . .

Bible in a year: Nehemiah 3,4; Luke 6

Wednesday 10 July
Acts 7:35–53

Ever-present God

PREPARE
'Better is one day in your courts than a thousand elsewhere' (Psalm 84:10). Reflect on what this means to you.

. . . .

READ
Acts 7:35–53

EXPLORE
As Stephen reaches the end of his retelling of Israel's history, we realise what he has been doing: he has been showing how God's chosen people have always rejected his messengers (vs 9,25,39). Stephen had carried his listeners with him up to this point. But then he turns on them in verses 52 and 53, showing that their rejection and crucifixion of Jesus followed the pattern set by their ancestors.

Stephen also reminds them that God is always present with his people. He was there at the foot of the mountain while he talked with Moses at the summit (vs 38–42). God was present in the tabernacle as they travelled through the wilderness (v 44) and settled in the Promised Land (v 45). David wanted to build a Temple and his son Solomon ultimately did so (vs 46,47). But Stephen points out that the Temple was always a symbol of God's presence (vs 48–50): if it

were taken away, God would still be with his people. Stephen had been accused of saying that Jesus would destroy the Temple (6:14). Some of those present may have lived to see it destroyed by the Romans in AD 70. But Stephen's words are a reminder that God is still with us even when physical symbols are gone.

'You stiff-necked people! Your hearts and ears are still uncircumcised. You are just like your ancestors: you always resist the Holy Spirit!'
Acts 7:51

RESPOND
Don't rush away! Still your mind and your heart. Take time to remember that God is present. Throughout the day, keep reminding yourself that the Lord of the universe is with you.

. . . .

Bible in a year: Nehemiah 5,6; Luke 7

Calm in the storm

PREPARE
Thank Jesus for his sacrifice for you on the cross.

READ
Acts 7:54 – 8:8

EXPLORE
This is a dramatic moment for the church. Stephen's sermon makes the people so angry that they drive him out of the city and stone him (v 58). Amid the noise, the anger, the shouting, the violence, Stephen himself appears to be like the calm eye of the storm. He is transfixed by a vision of Jesus (7:55) and prays for his killers (v 60), just as Jesus had done on the cross (Luke 23:34). Contrast that with the possible raging anger evident in 'a young man named Saul' (7:58; 8:1,3). Saul is zealous in his pursuit of Jesus' followers, going house to house and throwing people into jail.

The persecution in Jerusalem causes believers to flee in different directions (8:1). However, they are not running away to find the best hiding places nor disappearing into the shadows. No, they preach as they go (8:4) and their preaching draws crowds (8:6). They leave because they can do more good free than in jail.

It has been a privilege for me personally to live and travel in post-communist Europe and to listen to the recollections of Christians who faced very real persecution. I have not experienced that first-hand, so I cannot say for sure how I would react. But here in the UK Christian beliefs are increasingly under attack both in the social sphere and in workplaces.

> Those who had been scattered preached the word wherever they went.
>
> **Acts 8:4**

RESPOND
Pray that those facing persecution in their nation or in their workplace would know whether to stay or to go.

Bible in a year: Nehemiah 7,8; Luke 8

Friday 12 July
Acts 8:9–25

Changing sides

PREPARE
Pray for friends and relatives who don't yet know Jesus.

READ
Acts 8:9–25

EXPLORE

Having worked wonders himself, Simon was fascinated by the miracles the disciples performed (v 13). He just couldn't get enough of them. And if that spiritual power drew him, the ability to give power to others was irresistible (v 18). While he had made an outward confession of faith, his thoughts and heart were still catching up, trapped in the values of his old way of life.

I wish I knew the end of the story. What happened to Simon (v 24)? Did he go on to mature in his faith? Or did he return to his earlier magic? The fact that we don't know is probably a good thing. In our own efforts to convert and disciple new believers, we see both positive and negative outcomes. What we learn from the disciples is first to do all we can to support a person's declaration of faith (v 13). Secondly, we see Philip allowing Simon to tag along and gain experience (v 13). Next, Peter is very direct with Simon when he has made a massive error (vs 20–23). Peter is also teaching him here that repentance should be personal and that he needs to pray. We can read Simon's response in verse 24 as genuine repentance and a cry for mentoring and spiritual support, so perhaps another lesson is the importance of discipleship.

> Simon himself believed and was baptised. And he followed Philip everywhere, astonished by the great signs and miracles he saw.
>
> **Acts 8:13**

RESPOND
Pray for anyone you know who has recently come to faith. Pray that they would both develop their own relationship with the Lord and have good mentors.

Bible in a year: Nehemiah 9,10; Psalm 78:38–72

Led by the Lord

PREPARE

As we reach the end of this series in Acts, what has God taught you?

● ●

READ

Acts 8:26-40

EXPLORE

Reading this, I can't help thinking about Jonah! God said to Jonah, 'Go!' and he ran in the opposite direction (Jonah 1:1-3). God said to Philip, 'Go!' and he set out immediately (vs 26,27), only knowing that he was supposed to go south. We're not told how he feels about it. He has just fled Jerusalem because of the persecution (v 5) and his ministry is going really well in the town he's stopped in (vs 6,7). It can't have been easy to walk away from this successful urban ministry that's drawing crowds and head down 'the desert road' (v 26).

Having been obedient to that first command, he is given a little more detail (v 29). He is listening to the Spirit's voice for further instruction and immediately obeys. After that, he simply takes the opportunities that arise, offering to explain the Scriptures to the Ethiopian (v 30), climbing into the carriage when invited (v 31) and then baptising the man when they reach water (v 38).

Philip is spontaneous, but he is also prepared. He is ready to explain the gospel message from whatever passage he hears (v 35). Clearly, he had spent time studying the Scriptures and listening to the apostles' teaching so that he was ready to give an answer (1 Peter 3:15). So Philip is obedient, spontaneous and prepared – which of those do you find hardest?

> Then Philip began with that very passage of Scripture and told him the good news about Jesus.

Acts 8:35

RESPOND

Pray that God would lead you into opportunities to share his message.

● ●

Bible in a year: Nehemiah 11,12; Luke 9

Sunday 14 July
Psalm 144

Confident hope

PREPARE
What struggles are you facing currently? Bring them to the Lord and ask for his help.

....

READ
Psalm 144

EXPLORE
As a king who has fought so many battles, David longs and prays for his people that the next generation (v 12) will live in peace. His hope is that they will be able to go about their business without the threat of being attacked or taken captive (v 14). He is confident that this will indeed be their future because of who their God is (v 15).

David himself, though, is still at war. The words he uses to describe God in verse 2 are wonderful: but they are all things that you only need during a battle. David is confident about the outcome because he has confidence in his God. In verses 2 to 6 we see David meditating on the strength and greatness of God and left in awe at the fact that such a God would be in relationship with him (vs 3,4).

He asks God to intervene miraculously (vs 6,7), but also expects to have to do some of the fighting (v 1). When we face our own battles, do we ask God to train us to fight as often as we ask him to change the circumstances or miraculously remove the threat?

He is my loving God and my fortress, my stronghold and my deliverer, my shield, in whom I take refuge.

Psalm 144:2

RESPOND
David describes God as his rock, his fortress, his stronghold, his deliverer... How many more words can you think of to describe who God is for you? Use them as a basis for your praise now.

....

Bible in a year: Nehemiah 13; Luke 10

The long road of faith

About the writer
Steve Silvester

Steve is Rector of St Nic's Nottingham, a thriving, international, city-centre church. With his wife Jane, he is also a foster carer. In 2015, he founded Nottingham City Prayer, uniting churches across the city. Steve is a keen road cyclist and walker.

Eugene Peterson described the Christian life as 'a long obedience in the same direction'.* In reality, for many of us, the journey has many twists and turns. Sometimes it is difficult to keep going as the promised destination slips below the horizon. We may even feel like giving up. How can we keep believing when circumstances and society challenge faith so relentlessly?

In this series we will retrace Abraham's archetypal journey of faith. It's no secret that the story ends with the birth of Isaac, the promised child. However, we will conclude the series before this happens and focus on the journey itself. It is full of hopes raised and dashed, deviations from the course God had in mind, and faith strained almost to breaking point. But it is also a journey of maturing faith, deepening understanding of the ways of God and perseverance.

You may be finding that life is not working out as you expected. You may be living with unanswered prayers, dashed hopes and faith so stretched that it is starting to fray. Equally, you may be sprinting forward at the start of your journey with God and need to be prepared for the marathon that lies ahead.

Whatever your situation, I pray that this very human story of Abraham and Sarah will encourage you and help you to know that you are not alone. God is faithful, and we can be too.

*Eugene H Peterson, *A Long Obedience in the Same Direction*, IVP, 1980

Monday 15 July
Genesis 12:1–9

Who do you think you are?

PREPARE
Read 1 John 3:2. Allow God to remind you of who you really are, through Jesus. Can you offer yourself again to become all that he wants you to be?

READ
Genesis 12:1–9

EXPLORE

The popular British TV show *Who Do You Think You Are?* takes a celebrity into their family history. The title implies that your past explains who you are. You are the sum of your history.

Abram's family history, given in Genesis 11, dominates our introduction to Abram. His life is dictated by his father, who inexplicably makes the decision to leave Ur, the centre of civilisation in the ancient Middle East, planning to take his entire family to Canaan (Genesis 11:31). Abram has no choice. His past is his destiny.

Genesis 12 changes everything. The call of God sets Abram on the path to become the father of all who have faith in God (Romans 4:11). He starts a life not predetermined by his father or ancestors, but by the call of God (12:1). He will leave behind his country, his people and his father's household. He is an ordinary man, but his response to God's call gives his life enduring significance. Interestingly, the journey begins with a call to move further in the direction his father has already begun to take him (v 5) – God was already at work in his family.

> The LORD had said to Abram, 'Go from your country, your people and your father's household to the land I will show you.'
>
> **Genesis 12:1**

RESPOND
Read John 1:11–13. Our identity and destiny depend not on our past but on our response to Jesus now. Is there anything you need to leave behind in order to wholeheartedly embrace God's call?

Bible in a year: Esther 1–3; Psalm 79

Instant jeopardy

PREPARE

What are your current worries and concerns? Why not jot them down now? Hear the invitation of God's Word to you: 'Cast all your anxiety on him [God] because he cares for you' (1 Peter 5:7).

READ

Genesis 12:10-20

EXPLORE

After the dramatic opening to the chapter, and God's amazing promises, everything threatens to fall apart immediately. Natural disaster, enforced migration, perceived threat from an alien regime and, perhaps most importantly, Abram's flawed character all conspire to undermine God's promised future. This is a recurring pattern in Abram's story. Time and again, dramatic twists make us wonder whether God's purposes will ever be fulfilled.

Psychologists tell us that we respond to perceived threat in one of five ways: fight, flight, freeze, fawn or flop. Fawning is defined as 'people-pleasing, even to your own detriment'. This is Abram's response to a threat that has not even been verified. He dissembles, placing his wife in danger to preserve himself. Pharaoh emerges from this story with better moral credentials than Abram.

This shows me that God's call is not dependent on our character. Rather, character is formed over time as we learn to act in response to God's call, and to trust him through all the unforeseen threats that could make us lose sight of his promises.

> 'When the Egyptians see you, they will say, "This is his wife." Then they will kill me but will let you live.'
>
> **Genesis 12:12**

RESPOND

Pray: 'Lord, you know me through and through. And still, you call me to walk the path of faith with you. As I follow you – and also, as I stumble or stray – please shape me to be the person you made me to be.'

Bible in a year: Esther 4,5; Luke 11

Wednesday 17 July
Genesis 13:1–18

Back and beyond

PREPARE
Spend a few moments looking back and thanking God for significant moments in your spiritual life.

READ
Genesis 13:1–18

EXPLORE
'Take her and go!' (Genesis 12:19). With these words of Pharaoh ringing in his ears, Abram leaves Egypt and moves into an unknown future. What now? He returns to a place that holds huge spiritual significance for him, Bethel, and again he 'calls on the name of the LORD' (13:4; 12:8). This is always a good thing to do in times of change and uncertainty. In order to move on with our Lord, we have to return to him. God, however, is not calling Abram backwards, but forwards into a deeper trust.

How will God's promise to Abram be fulfilled? Perhaps it will be through Lot, his nephew. Since the death of his father Haran (11:28), Abraham has been his guardian and, in some Jewish traditions, his adopted father.

This episode in Abram's life is often read as an example of unselfishness and faith, as he allows Lot to choose the best pasture, trusting that God will provide.

It is a generous gesture. However, the challenge to Abram comes in verse 15: will he trust God that the land he surveys will be given to his 'seed', his natural offspring?

> So Abram went to live near the great trees of Mamre at Hebron, where he pitched his tents. There he built an altar to the LORD.
>
> **Genesis 13:18**

RESPOND
Having returned to Bethel, Abram moves on and builds an altar at Mamre. This would become a place of even greater significance (Genesis 18). Is God calling you to move beyond the spiritual landmarks in your past and to trust him in a new way?

Bible in a year: Esther 6,7; Luke 12

Involved but not embroiled

PREPARE

What circumstances, relationships or world developments are affecting you against your will? Offer them to God and seek his wisdom.

READ

Genesis 14:1–24

EXPLORE

How do we live faithfully in a complex and unpredictable world? Abram and Sarai, far from being a solitary couple with a few sheep, have become significant players in their neighbourhood, able to muster a fighting force of 318 fighting men. As the political situation around them shifts, and as their relative Lot is carried off by invading forces, they cannot help but get involved. They have to take sides.

This episode concludes with the mysterious figure of Melchizedek, a king and priest, blessing Abram (vs 18–20). Melchizedek is presented as a priest of God Most High who recognises that, through all the unpredictability of life, God's blessing is on Abram, especially in his victory over the invading kings.

Abram receives this blessing. He doesn't imply that Melchizedek knows nothing about the true God. In fact, he honours his priesthood with a tithe. However, he distances himself from Melchizedek in two ways. In his subsequent conversation with the king of Sodom, he makes it known that he has further revelation about God. Secondly, he avoids opportunism, trusting that the blessing God has promised will come directly from himself without the favours of the pagan king of Sodom.

'... I will accept nothing belonging to you ... so that you will never be able to say, "I made Abram rich."'

Genesis 14:23

RESPOND

'Show me the way I should go, for to you I entrust my life' (Psalm 143:8).

Bible in a year: Esther 8–10; Luke 13

Let's get serious

PREPARE
As you come into prayer, how does your relationship with God stand?

· ·

READ
Genesis 15:1–21

EXPLORE
A covenant is a solemn undertaking. Today, covenants are used in marriage, making a will, finance, law and real estate. There are severe consequences when a covenant is broken. The seriousness of God's covenant with Abram is expressed in the strange ritual in which animals and birds are cut in half and the blazing torch, representing God's presence, passes between the pieces. In effect, God is saying, 'May I be like these animals if I do not keep to this covenant.'

This is the second covenant mentioned in the Bible. The first (Genesis 9) is with Noah, representing all humanity, and 'every living creature'. It is God's commitment to his creation. The covenant with Abram is personal, the cementing of a relationship which has developed since God first called Abram in chapter 12, through which all humanity will be blessed.

You may wonder, 'Why does God commit to one man, to one tribe, to one nation?' The personal nature of this covenant tells us something important about God. He loves with particularity. If my wife were to ask me, 'Do you love me?' and I were to reply, 'Of course I love you: I love all women,' she may not be very pleased. In the same way, God does not just love 'everyone'. He loves you, and me, and him, and her and them.

> On that day the Lord made a covenant with Abram...
>
> **Genesis 15:18**

RESPOND
Take some time to thank God for his commitment to you in Jesus (2 Corinthians 1:20). Do you want to renew your commitment to him?

· ·

Bible in a year: Job 1,2; Psalm 80

Tired of waiting

PREPARE
'Be still before the LORD and wait patiently for him' (Psalm 37:7). Be still now.

. . . .

READ
Genesis 16:1–16

EXPLORE
Waiting for God to fulfil his promises is hard. Eventually the strain begins to tell. It is human nature to want to nudge events towards fulfilment. While God takes his time, Abram has been weighing up the possibilities for succession – his nephew Lot or his servant Eliezer (15:2,3). It seems that Sarai has had enough of waiting and is desperate enough to share her husband with another woman, Hagar.

Waiting for God does not necessarily mean that we remain passive. Abram had clearly been busy. By now he is a wealthy man with a large, extended household. However, taking things into our own hands in order to 'help' God is never wise.

God's graciousness to Hagar is deeply touching. He attends to the messy consequences of Abram and Sarai's faltering trust with compassion and care.

You may be struggling to continue to trust God as he seems to be taking his time. You are not alone, and you are not the first. Rabbi Jonathan Sacks wrote:

'Faith is the ability to live with delay without losing trust in the promise; to experience disappointment without losing hope, to know that the road between the real and the ideal is long and yet be willing to undertake the journey.'*

She gave this name to the LORD who spoke to her: 'You are the God who sees me,' for she said, 'I have now seen the One who sees me.'

Genesis 16:13

RESPOND
Use Psalm 90 to pray with a long view of history, but with honesty and urgency.

*Rabbi Jonathan Sacks, *Covenant and Conversation*, Toby Press, 2019, p93

. . . .

Bible in a year: Job 3,4; Luke 14

Sunday 21 July
Psalm 145

Your kingdom come...

PREPARE

'The LORD reigns ...' (Psalm 93:1). So relax and celebrate that he is in charge!

. . . .

READ
Psalm 145

EXPLORE

I love this psalm. It is a beautiful declaration of the kingdom of God – how life is meant to be and, ultimately, will be. It is a celebration of what should have been the glory of ancient Israel, and foretells the kingdom brought about by Jesus. God's rule is eternal, but constantly requires expression in the world. Notice how the psalmist talks about the timeless majesty of God and also commits to playing his part in his generation: 'They tell ... and I will meditate ... They tell ... and I will proclaim' (vs 4–6).

So what are the distinctive features of the kingdom of God? There are, of course, God's power and majesty (vs 1–6), but there are many aspects that would not be shared by some regimes of the ancient world or of today. Compassion is a key feature (vs 8,9). God's kingdom is a place where the weak are treated with special care. Unlike so many governments, God exercises power for his subjects, not just over them. He is responsive to the cry of the needy (vs 14–16).

There is a place for judgement in God's kingdom, though this only merits half a verse (v 20). This has to be the case if the weak are to be defended and if 'every creature' (v 21) is to thrive.

Your kingdom is an everlasting kingdom, and your dominion endures through all generations.
Psalm 145:13

RESPOND

Jesus teaches us to pray, 'Your kingdom come, your will be done, on earth...' Let this psalm guide you as you pray for our world.

. . . .

Bible in a year: Job 5,6; Luke 15

Flip side of covenant

PREPARE

Read 2 Timothy 2:11–13. Thank God for his faithfulness to you and ask him to help you to remain faithful to him, whatever challenges you face.

READ

Genesis 17:1–16

EXPLORE

When God made his covenant with Abram in chapter 15, Abram was passive. As the covenant was ritually sealed, Abram was in a deep sleep and covered with 'a thick and dreadful darkness'. The covenant is entirely God's initiative.

However, a covenant is between two parties and here we see Abram's side. This involved the rite of circumcision for Abram and a change of name for him (v 5) and Sarai (v 15). Many societies practise circumcision as a transition into manhood. Abram's circumcision does not say, 'I have arrived.' It says, 'I am fully committed to receive all you have for me' (v 11).

Through Jesus, we have a 'new covenant' with God (Luke 22:20). Again, this is entirely God's initiative (eg Ephesians 2:1–5). The Old and New Testaments are consistent: in mercy, kindness and unmerited grace, God takes the initiative. However, there is a human side to the covenant, which is faith. The New Testament emphasises that God always engages with humanity in this way (see Romans 4). As Christians we can be 'ministers of the new covenant' (2 Corinthians 3:6), having a ministry of reconciliation (2 Corinthians 5:18), sharing God's initiative and inviting others into a covenant relationship with him.

Then God said to Abraham, 'As for you, you must keep my covenant, you and your descendants after you for the generations to come.'
Genesis 17:9

RESPOND

Thank God that 'When you were dead in your sins and in the uncircumcision of your flesh, God made you alive with Christ. He forgave us all our sins' (Colossians 2:13).

Bible in a year: Job 7,8; Psalms 81,82

Tuesday 23 July
Genesis 17:17–27

Wide mercy

PREPARE
Use Ephesians 2:4–10 to thank God for his kindness to you.

READ
Genesis 17:17–27

EXPLORE

Abraham might well laugh (v 17). At the age of 99 he is 'as good as dead' (Hebrews 11:12). But God has not finished with him – his promise is yet to be fulfilled through a son to be born to Sarah. Can't God see that he has a perfectly good heir in Ishmael? God seems to be driving intentionally towards the brink of impossibility. If Abraham is to be the father of faith, he must reach a point where it is 'God or bust'.

However, in the words of the hymnwriter FW Faber, 'There's a wideness in God's mercy' (1854). Although God insists that his covenant will continue through Sarah's son (v 21), his grace and kindness can reach to Ishmael. As if not to miss this extraordinary opportunity, Abraham wastes no time in getting Ishmael circumcised, along with himself and the rest of his household, even those who came as slaves from foreigners. He wants as many as possible to be included in the covenant.

I wonder if I share God's (and Abraham's) instinct for generosity. Sometimes, I fear that I am like Jonah who, when he finally goes to the people of Nineveh, says resentfully, 'I *knew* that you are a gracious and compassionate God, slow to anger and abounding in love…' (Jonah 4:2). He's actually disappointed that God has been so kind!

> And Abraham said to God, 'If only Ishmael might live under your blessing!'
>
> **Genesis 17:18**

RESPOND
Are there people you secretly hope will be excluded from the scope of God's kindness? Ask God to soften your heart.

Bible in a year: Job 9,10; Luke 16

You must be joking!

PREPARE

Take some time to reflect on the people you have met, or will meet, today. How can you receive them in the name of Jesus? What gift may they bring you?

READ

Genesis 18:1–15

EXPLORE

What is going on here? Some Jewish interpreters of this text argue that while God is visiting Abraham (v 1) three strangers appear – and Abraham breaks off his conversation with God in order to welcome them. Thus, they say, 'Greater is hospitality than receiving the divine presence.'* This line of thinking continues in the New Testament: 'Whoever claims to love God yet hates a brother or sister is a liar. For whoever does not love their brother and sister, whom they have seen, cannot love God, whom they have not seen' (1 John 4:20).

Christian theologians have seen the three visitors as an amplification of God's appearance to Abraham, not as a separate incident. They argue that the text moves seamlessly between the three visitors and Yahweh (eg v 13). Famously, Rublev's icon depicts the three visitors as the Trinity.

One thing is clear. Through this incident God repeats his promise that a child will be born to Sarah. God speaks through three strangers, under a tree, following eastern hospitality. And yet so much time has elapsed, so many hopes have been raised and unfulfilled, that Sarah can only laugh at what she hears.

So Sarah laughed to herself as she thought, 'After I am worn out and my lord is old, will I now have this pleasure?'
Genesis 18:12

RESPOND

How may God want to speak to you today? Through others, even through strangers, his Word may come. Even when you have given up hope, he may be speaking. Pray: 'Lord, speak for I'm listening.'

*See, for example: www.rabbisacks.org/covenant-conversation/vayera/even-higher-than-angels/

Bible in a year: Job 11,12; Luke 17

Thursday 25 July
Genesis 18:16–33

Divine justice

PREPARE
'Consider ... the kindness and sternness of God' (Romans 11:22). How do you feel about these aspects of God's character?

READ
Genesis 18:16–33

EXPLORE

This remarkable conversation is the prelude to the judgement of Sodom, the home of Abraham's nephew Lot, legendary for its wickedness. If you have haggled in an eastern market, you will recognise Abraham's style. Is it OK to speak to God like this? It seems that the Lord positively invites Abraham to do so because his nature is always to have mercy.

Abraham is fiercely protective of his nephew, but being a descendant of Abraham requires more than ancestry. God's vision is that Abraham will raise a people who, from generation to generation, will 'keep the way of the Lord' (v 19; see Romans 9:8). Abraham himself needs to learn this way.

The way of the Lord involves 'doing what is right and just' (v 19), so in this situation how will 'the Judge of all the earth do right' (v 25)? The focus of this incident is

not so much Abraham trying to change God's mind as God teaching Abraham his mind. Justice is a struggle: both sides in the argument have to be represented. God welcomes Abraham's pleading, as the counsel for the defence, but ultimately justice will require a terrible judgement on the sinful cities. Only through the death of his Son can God both be just and justify sinful people (Romans 3:26).

> 'Will not the Judge of all the earth do right?'
>
> **Genesis 18:25**

RESPOND
'What does the Lord require of you? To act justly and to love mercy and to walk humbly with your God' (Micah 6:8). Are you meeting his requirements today?

Bible in a year: Job 13,14; Luke 18

As low as you can get

PREPARE
What does it mean to live as 'foreigners and exiles' in society? (See 1 Peter 2:11,12.)

READ
Genesis 19:1–14

EXPLORE
The Dead Sea is the lowest place on earth, 3,000 feet below sea level. Sodom and Gomorrah, probably located to its north, represent the lowest reaches of human depravity. This incident is described by Rabbi Jonathan Sacks as 'a multiple offence, involving: forbidden sex, violence, and a breach of the strict code of hospitality in the ancient Near East'.* It is presented as compounded evil, an 'outcry' (v 13).

Lot concentrates only on the breach of hospitality. He has chosen to make his home in Sodom, an outsider for whom social integration is of high value. Welcome and belonging are everything. It is as though he is blind to the other aspects of his neighbours' behaviour, and even to the outrageousness of his attempt to placate them by offering his daughters for gang rape.

Wanting to belong or fit in can easily distort our moral vision. Our attitudes and thinking can quickly become infected. We find ourselves tricked by false loyalties, compromised in our attempts to be accommodating and confused in understanding what is 'right and just'. Lot is so embroiled that he cannot find the will to leave this corrupting environment. And yet, if he doesn't leave, he will be 'swept away' with it (v 15).

'The outcry to the LORD against its people is so great that he has sent us to destroy it.'
Genesis 19:13

RESPOND
Is there a situation you need to remove yourself from, even if you are tempted to stay for the best of reasons? (See 2 Corinthians 6:14–18.)

*Rabbi Jonathan Sacks, *Covenant and Conversation*, Toby Press, 2019, p106

Bible in a year: Job 15–17; Psalms 83,84

Saturday 27 July
Genesis 19:15–29

Don't look back

PREPARE
Is your present more influenced by past regrets than future hope?

READ
Genesis 19:15–29

EXPLORE
Gone. The life they had built, the home they had made, the contacts they had fostered – all that Lot and his family had worked for was gone. It seems a small thing that Lot's wife should look over her shoulder as everything disappeared (v 26), but, as we have seen throughout this series, the life of faith is lived facing forwards. God's call to Abraham was to a future that had not yet materialised. In the New Testament, this theme is continued: 'For here we do not have an enduring city, but we are looking for the city that is to come' (Hebrews 13:14).

It is difficult to remain in this forward-facing attitude when all we hope for seems to continually slip over the horizon. For Christians, the life of faith is possible because we have received the foretaste, or down payment, guaranteeing the fulfilment of our hope. 'And hope does not put us to shame, because God's love has been poured out into our hearts through the Holy Spirit, who has been given to us' (Romans 5:5),

This series ends on a cliff-hanger. Behind is a scene of apocalyptic destruction. Ahead is God's promised future – a land, a family, a role in history – that can be accessed only through step-by-step trust in God's call. Lot does escape from Sodom, but he is unable to sustain the life of faith and his story ends shamefully (19:30–38). Abraham will journey on.

> But Lot's wife looked back, and she became a pillar of salt.

Genesis 19:26

RESPOND
Pray: 'To the past: Thanks. To the future: Yes' (Dag Hammarskjöld).

Bible in a year: Job 18,19; Luke 19

Worship and justice

PREPARE
'I love your Christ. It is just that so many of you Christians are so unlike your Christ' (Mahatma Gandhi). How does this statement speak to you?

. . . .

READ
Psalm 146

EXPLORE
'Faith by itself, if it is not accompanied by action, is dead' (James 2:17). This statement may seem to be an odd connection with this psalm, but the psalm has the same logic. It begins with a very familiar and general exclamation: 'Hallelujah!' Straight away, the psalmist makes a personal response to the truth: he summons his soul to praise the Lord, and declares that he will praise him through the whole of his life. He is going to act on what he knows to be true.

There are many reasons to praise the Lord, some of which are listed in verses 6 to 9. Our God is so different from other rulers (v 3). But all these qualities of God are not merely to be admired. They require action. The statement in the final verse, 'The LORD reigns for ever, your God, O Zion, for all generations', comes with the implication that Zion (Jerusalem) also needs to be a place where the cause of the oppressed is upheld, the hungry are fed, those who are bowed down are lifted up, and the foreigner and widow are treated with compassion and justice. Only then can God truly be said to reign in Zion.

I will praise the LORD all my life; I will sing praise to my God as long as I live.
Psalm 146:2

RESPOND
Talk to God about your worship life. Does praise rise readily from your heart? Is your worship evident in how you live as well as what you say or sing?

. . . .

Bible in a year: Job 20,21; Luke 20

Hard truths

From the beginning of his account of the life of Jesus, John focuses on Jesus' origins. The events he records illustrate that Jesus is human like us, but not like us: humans do not have the power to turn water into wine or multiply a few loaves and fish into a meal for 5,000! Neither do people make the sort of claims that Jesus made (judge over everything, John 5:22,27; with power to give life to the dead, John 5:21,24). If they did, they would soon be referred to a psychiatrist! Indeed, in our readings this week, we'll see the Jews reacting strongly against Jesus' claims.

The burning question for the Jews then and for people today is: Can we trust what Jesus says? What are his credentials? Who is he really? John 8 touches on all these questions as we listen in on Jesus acting as judge, confronting the Jews with the truth about them and about himself.

Although the verses of John 8:1–11 are not found in the earliest manuscripts (which is why they may appear in italics in your Bible), the scene follows a recurring theme in John's Gospel: Jesus the judge who confronts people with the truth (see John 4:16–18; 5:14,15). The incident gives us a glimpse of a judge who upholds truth and holiness but whose heart is full of mercy. That beautiful combination of justice and mercy would ultimately take Jesus to the cross.

About the writer
Penny Boshoff

Penny is a teacher and a writer. She currently teaches English as a Foreign Language to primary aged children. She enjoys helping adults, teenagers and young children explore the Bible together in small groups.

Trapped

PREPARE
One day we will stand before God, judge of all. How we approach that day depends on how well we know our judge. Ask God to help you know him better.

. . . .

READ
John 8:2-11

EXPLORE
The Jewish teachers had devised a cunning plan to trap Jesus: would Jesus – who had form in breaking the finer points of Sabbath regulations (see John 5:8) – uphold the law of Moses regarding sexual immorality? If he upheld Jewish law by permitting stoning, then he would be breaking Roman law since Jews had no legal right under Rome to exact the death penalty (see John 18:31). Either way, he would be breaking the law. Jesus' response is brilliant. He does not minimise the seriousness of sexual sin. He upholds the law of Moses and in the same breath he proves that the crowd are also trapped in sin.

The woman, trapped by the Jewish leaders (v 3) and by her own sin (v 11), stands before her judge: the only one who could legitimately throw a stone (see John 5:22). She had no idea that the mercy he offered her came at a great cost. Jesus' blood would be shed for her sin, just as it was shed for ours. What he offered the woman (v 11) is what he offers each of us: mercy and new life free from the law of sin and death (see Romans 8:1,2).

'Then neither do I condemn you,' Jesus declared. 'Go now and leave your life of sin.'
John 8:11

RESPOND
Praise Jesus for his perfect justice and his breathtakingly beautiful mercy.

. . . .

Bible in a year: Job 22,23; Psalm 85

Tuesday 30 July
John 8:12–20

Show me your credentials

PREPARE

Knowing about someone involves facts. Knowing someone involves relationship. Consider what you know about Jesus, then reflect on how you know him day to day.

READ

John 8:12–20

EXPLORE

Jesus makes his extraordinary and audacious claim (v 12) shortly after the Festival of Tabernacles when huge lamps were lit in the Temple courts. These lights reminded the Jews that God, in the form of a pillar of fire, had guided their ancestors from slavery in Egypt towards the Promised Land. In one short phrase, Jesus linked himself to the light of God's presence in that pillar of fire, and to God's initial act of creation (Genesis 1:3,4), creating light and separating it from darkness. No wonder the Pharisees question his claim and want to check his credentials (v 13).

The Pharisees, just like many people today, refuse to accept what Jesus had already told them about who he is and where he's from (see John 6:38,51). They fixate on earthly origins (vs 19; 7:41) and earthly witnesses while Jesus continually points them to his divine credentials (vs 14–18). For anyone questioning Jesus' credentials today, there is even more evidence (Jesus' resurrection and ascension) and more witnesses, both earthly and heavenly (see Luke 24:4–7; Acts 1:3; 1 Corinthians 15:3–8), to prove that Jesus is who he says he is!

> 'You do not know me or my Father,' Jesus replied. 'If you knew me, you would know my Father also.'
>
> **John 8:19**

RESPOND

Pray that the light of Jesus would give life to anyone struggling in darkness, and understanding to those who don't yet know him.

Bible in a year: Job 24–26; Luke 21

A dire prognosis

PREPARE
Pray: 'Restore to me the joy of your salvation and grant me a willing spirit, to sustain me. Then I will teach transgressors your ways, so that sinners will turn back to you' (Psalm 51:12,13).

READ
John 8:21–30

EXPLORE
If I suffer from a serious medical condition the sensible course of action is to consult a medical specialist, then act on their diagnosis by following their treatment plan.

Jesus delivers a very uncomfortable prognosis (vs 21,24): the sin disease, that affects every human, leads to death. But he also offers hope for anyone who follows his treatment plan: believe in Jesus (v 24) and you will receive eternal life (see John 3:16).

The problem was that the Jews did not trust their spiritual doctor. They could not countenance the possibility that Jesus had been sent from God's presence in heaven (vs 23,26; 5:17,18). Of course, if they accepted his claim to speak on behalf of God the Father (v 28), then they would need to listen to Jesus and act on his teaching.

So how can such sceptics change their minds? Jesus prophesies that understanding would come after he is 'lifted up' or exalted (v 28). At Pentecost, when Peter preached that Jesus died on the cross, was raised in resurrection and exalted in his ascension (Acts 2:22–36), many Jews changed their minds and believed.

'I told you that you would die in your sins; if you do not believe that I am he, you will indeed die in your sins.'

John 8:24

RESPOND
Ask God for opportunities and the boldness to speak of Jesus' death, resurrection and ascension with sceptical friends and family members.

Bible in a year: Job 27,28; Luke 22

Thursday 1 August
John 8:31–41

Trapped by lies

PREPARE
Come to your heavenly Father to confess your sin: 'According to your unfailing love ... Wash away all my iniquity and cleanse me from my sin' (Psalm 51:1,2).

• •

READ
John 8:31–41

EXPLORE
Jesus' claim that following his teaching leads to truth and that this can set us free (v 32), has never been more relevant. When 'fake news' conspiracy theories and 'deep fake' photos and video clips abound then our view of the world becomes distorted: we don't know what is true or who to trust. We may not even be aware that we are trapped, 'slaves' to the lie.

The lie that Jesus exposes here is the one that convinces us that family or cultural affiliation makes us right with God. The Jews thought that, as descendants of Abraham, they were automatically God's children (vs 33,39). In the same way people now might assume they are Christian because their parents were, or they grew up in a 'Christian' country. Belonging to God's family is not passed down in DNA, in cultural institutions nor even in attending church regularly.

To dispel the lie, we must accept the uncomfortable truth (v 34). Our thoughts and attitudes to Jesus (vs 37,40) show where we truly are. The Jews couldn't free themselves, and neither can we. Only Jesus can set us free (v 36).

> 'Very truly I tell you, everyone who sins is a slave to sin ... So if the Son sets you free, you will be free indeed.'
> **John 8:34,36**

RESPOND
Thank God for your freedom from sin, and for the gift of his Spirit within you, assuring you that you are truly his child (see Romans 8:14–16).

• •

Bible in a year: Job 29,30; Luke 23

Catch-22

PREPARE
Pray: 'Father God, give us today the Spirit of wisdom and revelation so that we may know you better. Amen.'

READ
John 8:42–47

EXPLORE
Jesus addresses these words to people who had seen his miracles and chosen to believe him (v 31), but according to Jesus they were unable to grasp their dire spiritual condition and their need for Jesus to set them free (vs 33,43). Do you ever wonder why some people hear the good news but seem to be impervious to it? Or why some people revere Jesus as a moral teacher but react angrily to the suggestion that they are sinners?

According to Jesus, only those who belong to God can hear and understand (v 47). It seems an impossible situation, a catch-22!

The reason people do not understand is because they are held captive by the devil, caught in his web of lies and unable to recognise and respond to the truth (vs 43–45). It is a hard truth to hear that every person is held prisoner by sin and the devil (v 34; see Psalm 14:1–3;

2 Corinthians 4:4), unable to hear the voice of God. The only way out of this catch-22 is through Jesus (v 36). So let's keep talking about Jesus to those who appear deaf to him, trusting God to work in their hearts.

'Whoever belongs to God hears what God says. The reason you do not hear is that you do not belong to God.'
John 8:47

RESPOND
Thank God for setting you free from sin then pray for someone who does not yet belong to him.

Bible in a year: Job 31,32; Psalms 86,87

Saturday 3 August
John 8:48–59

Deserving of honour

PREPARE
Honour Jesus now in prayer. Think of all he has accomplished for you. Give him praise and thanks.

READ
John 8:48–59

EXPLORE

How do we respond when we are confronted with unpalatable truths? Do we weigh the comments with humble self-reflection, or do we lash out? The Jews responded with insults (v 48)! The Samaritans were of mixed ethnicity and worshipped on their own sacred mountain instead of in Jerusalem, so the Jews' use of the word 'Samaritan' insulted Jesus' Jewishness and implied he was a heretic. Jesus overlooks the personal attack but takes issue with the insult (v 49) that dishonoured the Spirit of God within him.

Jesus claims they should honour him because God the Father desires it (vs 50,54), because he knows God better than they do (v 55) and because he has power over death (v 51).

Each of these is shockingly audacious, but the statement that most riled his listeners was Jesus' claim to precede Abraham and his use of the name of God in the phrase 'before Abraham was born, I am!' (v 58; see Exodus 3:14). Jesus was effectively claiming to be God. For the Jews this was blasphemy warranting the death penalty (v 59), which only proved that Jesus, the true judge, had been right about them all along (vs 40,44)!

> 'My Father, whom you claim as your God, is the one who glorifies me.'
> **John 8:54**

RESPOND
What do we do when people insult Jesus? Do we remind them of who Jesus claimed to be and why he deserves our honour, or do we keep silent?

Bible in a year: Job 33,34; Luke 24

Praise God

PREPARE
Offer your own song of praise to God or listen to 'How good it is to sing', which is based on Psalm 147.* Or, read aloud...

READ
Psalm 147

EXPLORE
This is a song written for those returning to Israel following their 70 years in exile in Babylon. Jerusalem is still in ruins (v 2), the people still carry the mental and emotional scars from their time in Babylon (vs 3,6), but their years of exile have given them a greater appreciation for God (see 2 Chronicles 36:21–23), whom they had previously taken for granted. Their return is a sign of God's continuing goodness, power and love (vs 5,11).

How has your love for God and appreciation for his goodness grown through tough times? Perhaps you wandered away from God for a time, but he has gathered (v 2) you back into his people, the church. Reflect on the times he has 'bound up your wounds', restoring you and comforting you. In what ways has he provided for you (vs 8,9)? When has he given you the security and space you needed to thrive (vs 13,14)?

The returning exiles had a new appreciation for their unique relationship with God (vs 19, 20)! Hebrews 1:2 declares that we have an even greater privilege ('... in these last days he has spoken to us by his Son'). Is it one we take for granted?

> The LORD delights in those who fear him, who put their hope in his unfailing love.

Psalm 147:11

RESPOND
Use the questions within our reflection today to build your own personal list of praise for what God has done in your life and in your community.

*www.youtube.com/watch?v=o8bn2sM97A8

Bible in a year: Job 35,36; Philippians 1

The Bible and me –
a writer's experience of the Bible

In these Spotlight articles, we ask *Daily Bread* writers to tell us a little about what the Bible means to them. For this issue we talked with **Penny Boshoff**.

What were your early experiences of the Bible?

As a young child, two of my favourite picture books taught me about Jesus. One was a delightful retelling of Jesus welcoming children of different ages. The other was a whimsical, yet profoundly wise, book which began: 'If Jesus came to my house and knocked upon the door, I'm sure I'd be more happy than I've ever been before' and showed a child happily playing with the boy Jesus in different rooms of the house. That was the relationship I wanted with Jesus too.

How did your appreciation of the Bible grow as you got older?

Looking back, I realise that much of my love and respect for the Bible came from the example of the adults who surrounded me. I recall my mum reading stories from our children's picture Bible and later giving me a copy of SU's Bible reading notes for children. From that point onwards, I became a Bible reader.

One holiday, my great aunt and uncle invited me, aged 11, along to their church Bible study. That simple invitation taught me that my faith and relationship with God were important and that I was welcome to learn alongside adults. When my own church began a weekly evening Bible study, I went with my mum.

Our Bible teacher, Mr Chapman, brought the Old and New Testaments to life and modelled how to approach a Bible passage by considering its historical context and its place in the overarching story of Israel and the church. In that group any question and contribution was welcomed. There I learned that exploring the Bible as a community, listening to one another and learning from one another, helps us all grow in our relationship with God.

Our church encouraged everyone to have their own Bible and to read it during the week. Everyone was expected to bring their Bible to church to check that what the preacher said matched what the Bible said! I was impressed by members of the church who quoted knowledgably from the Bible, but was drawn more to those who gripped their well-thumbed, threadbare Bibles with an excitement and passion, expecting God to speak to them. Some of those people worked for Open Doors and would regularly leave on trips taking Bibles to Christians behind the iron curtain. They recounted how East European Christians valued God's Word more than their personal safety. Such passion for the Bible taught me that what was in its pages was of immense and eternal value – infinitely precious!

A slow, steady work of transformation...

Those principles that I learned as a child and teenager have deepened over the years as I discover more of God's beautiful character by reading the Bible each day. Like an intricate tapestry or a complex and compelling piece of music, there are key themes, truths about God and about humanity that weave through the different books of the Bible. The more I read it, the more connections and patterns I see which only makes me want to discover more!

About 15 years ago I realised how contemporary culture, the news and media were influencing me in subtle ways. I took Romans 12:2 as a verse for the year, meditating on it again and again, praying that the Lord would transform my mind. That experience convinced me of the benefit of savouring God's Word, giving it time to settle in my mind and heart. We often want a fast fix, but I have discovered that God sometimes does a slow, steady work of transformation.

The Bible writers often compare God's Word to food. Just as we need a regular intake of food to keep our bodies functioning, so we need a regular intake of scripture. For me, my morning Bible reading is like a spiritual breakfast and a deep Bible study with other Christians is like a delicious Sunday lunch with family!

Over the years there have been thrilling times when God has spoken directly through a passage into my own situation. Other times, reading the Bible has been like travelling through a desert. At those times, discipline is my friend! As I continue to read the Scriptures and pray, the Lord is always faithful, bringing me out of those spiritual 'deserts' with more insight into his character and his ways than I had before.

Penny Boshoff

FREE MISSION SUPPORT

ᕈ Scripture Union

Unlock the full potential of your outreach to children and young people with **FREE** Mission Support from Scripture Union.

· ·

Sign up today for inspiration and advice from experienced professionals:

su.org.uk/missionsupport

WE'D BE GREAT TOGETHER

The next generation

My grandfather moved to London from Liverpool in 1920 to work as a taxman. The first Sunday he went to church where he espied an attractive young woman in the choir. They fell in love, got married and brought up their children to know and love God. Their daughter (my mum) brought up her daughters to put their trust in God. They, in their turn, nurtured the Christian faith of their children who now teach their children the wonders of God.

About the writer
Ro Willoughby

For many years Ro was a commissioning editor with Scripture Union. Now a lay minister in St Chad's Woodseats, Sheffield, she enjoys the many benefits of life in Sheffield, which include the company of family, friends, neighbours and fellow pilgrims.

Each generation within individual families, or society's label for a span of 20 years, is shaped by shared life events and shifting cultural or social values. Each generation encounters God for themselves, choosing what to believe and value. Hearing stories of family or societal folklore is never enough. God's invitation to be in relationship with him remains unchanged.

During the period of the Judges (around 1300–1050 BC), Israel only remained faithful to God for brief periods. They compromised, choosing to reject him by worshipping the false gods of their neighbours. It spelled disaster! One reason for this was the failure to pass the knowledge of God's covenant love down the generations. The responsibility of each generation is expressed in Psalm 78:4,6,7:

'We will tell the next generation the praiseworthy deeds of the LORD, his power, and the wonders he has done … so that the next generation would know them, even the children yet to be born … Then they would put their trust in God…'

Monday 5 August
Judges 2:6–23

Under God's covenant

PREPARE

What promises have you made, both recently and in the distant past? What helped you keep them?

. . . .

READ

Judges 2:6–23

EXPLORE

God made a covenant with Abraham, the founding father of the people of Israel. Once the Israelites were freed from Egypt, under the leadership of Moses, he made a second covenant, claiming them as his own and promising to bless them (Exodus 19:3–8). He called them to worship him faithfully, and him alone (Exodus 20:1–11).

Generations had come and gone. The stories of God's greatness and knowledge of this covenant may have been faithfully enough passed on to future generations. But then what happened (v 10)? Read verses 11–15 again to reflect on what followed as a result. Even God turned against them, as he had said he would (v 15).

Yet God remained faithful to his side of the covenant. Despite everything, he did not desert them but longed to draw them back to himself, using tough tactics (vs 20–22) so that they might follow him as earlier generations had done. He raised up leaders who oversaw a temporary relief. Notice, there's no mention here of anyone crying to God for mercy.

> But you are a chosen people … that you may declare the praises of him who called you out of darkness…

1 Peter 2:9

RESPOND

We live under the new covenant made possible by Christ's death and resurrection. God remains 100 per cent committed to it, with the result that '… now you are the people of God … now you have received mercy' (1 Peter 2:10). What in practice does this mean to you?

. . . .

Bible in a year: Job 37,38; Psalm 88

One inspiring leader

PREPARE

Which characters in the Bible inspire you? Thank God for their faith and what they achieved.

....

READ

Judges 4:1-24

EXPLORE

For centuries, the story of Deborah (but not Jael!) has continued to inspire, especially young girls. A sigh of relief must have greeted God's appointment of a new leader with a proven record of competence. But note, it took 20 years of cruel oppression before anyone cried out to God (v 3). They'd forgotten God's covenant with their ancestors!

Deborah is a woman who already has the authority to speak God's words (vs 5,6). Barak accepts her authority but not God's promise of victory. He won't go ahead without her (v 8). How often does the writer state that God wins the battle, not Barak? Two women transform the situation, one on the battlefield, one in a tent. Maybe Deborah's calm, inspirational reputation has been preserved with the help of her song in chapter 5. Jael on the other hand seals the victory. What motivates her to murder Sisera, the military commander

of Israel's arch enemy, King Jabin? We'll never know, but maybe Sisera had often visited her tent and she'd had enough of his unwelcome advances.

This is a story of God coming to the rescue, acting unexpectedly. Who could have expected God to take on human flesh?! Who can predict what God might do next? These are important truths about him to pass on.

> The mountains quaked before the LORD ... the God of Israel.
>
> **Judges 5:5**

RESPOND

Ask God's forgiveness for limiting your expectations of him. Pray with fresh confidence for God to intervene in apparently insoluble life situations.

....

Bible in a year: Job 39,40; Philippians 2

Feeling far from God?

PREPARE
Sometimes it seems God is absent. Perhaps we've turned from him, or maybe life events or mental health issues have caused us to feel desolate. What's your experience of this?

•••

READ
Judges 6:1–24

EXPLORE
Out of nowhere a prophet, a bit like John the Baptist, turns up. His message reminds the people of God's acts in history and points out that worshipping other gods is sin (vs 7–10). Gideon's generation has no excuse for ignorance.

Gideon shows he is familiar with his ancestors' history (v 13). But when an angel of the Lord sits down next to him, he accuses God of not providing for his people as he has done in the past. He blames God for the Midianites' assault on Israel, failing to recognise his people's sinful behaviour (v 1). He then contradicts the Lord, claiming to be too weak to lead Israel into battle successfully (v 15). He does not trust God to remain faithful, nor does he trust God's word and strength. But God is patient with Gideon (vs 16–24).

Here are important lessons for us. God never leaves us, even though it may feel like it. If he is being disobeyed, sin has to be identified and named. Yet, if we are feeling distant from God, we can cry out to him to make himself known. If we are feeling weak, he can make us strong (vs 14,16).

'I said to you, "I am the LORD your God; do not worship the gods of the Amorites, in whose land you live." But you have not listened to me.'

Judges 6:10

RESPOND
Feeling desolate? Talk with God – 'The LORD Is Peace' (v 24), however far away he seems. Pray for anyone you know who is feeling far from God.

•••

Bible in a year: Job 41,42; Philippians 3

The problems of a fleece

PREPARE

The phrase 'laying out a fleece', associated with Gideon's unorthodox decision-making, has passed into common use over generations. How do you involve God when seeking guidance?

READ

Judges 6:25–40

EXPLORE

Gideon continues to have doubts about God's instructions, but has no doubt that it's God speaking to him. His confidence has grown. He destroys his father's altar to Baal, a bold, irreversible action, though he does it under cover of darkness (v 27). He calls the tribes of the north to join him in battle, which they do. The Spirit of the Lord comes upon him (v 34). But then he gets cold feet, so seeks further reassurances of victory – assisted by a fleece (vs 36–38).

I've only once 'laid out a fleece'. With a big decision to make, we asked God to intervene within a week. On day seven a distant aunt rang me. We spoke briefly about God, then she rang off. Weeks after we'd made our decision I wondered if that was God's response! In Gideon's case, God had given him good reasons to be confident, but he generously played along with Gideon's fears and doubt.

I've never before told anyone about that day seven. But over the years I have passed on to the next generation far better stories about God's guidance and generosity to me. After all, it was Gideon's courage in obeying God and destroying the altar that established his reputation – and gave him a new name (v 32) – rather than the fleece!

Gideon said to God ... 'Allow me one more test with the fleece,' ... That night God did so.

Judges 6:39,40

RESPOND

Pray for an opportunity to tell someone a story of God's generosity towards you.

Bible in a year: Mark 1; Philippians 4

Safety in numbers?

PREPARE

What is your experience of being in a small minority, or a lone Christian? Ask God to help you engage emotionally with Gideon's acts of obedience.

READ

Judges 7:1–15

EXPLORE

32,000 soldiers is a large number of soldiers. This response to the call to the northern tribes to fight shows just how fearful they are. So great, that when invited to leave the battleground, two-thirds of them stand down (v 3). However, 10,000 remains significantly large. But to reduce it to 300 is sheer madness, though the troops are left with plenty of provisions (v 8). By this time Gideon does what God tells him to do. God even allows him to overhear the dream of a Midianite soldier and its subsequent interpretation as an additional encouragement. But note, this is the last recorded occasion when Gideon worships the Lord (v 15a).

Many stories in the Bible are about God's people in a tiny minority facing opposition – David on the run, Elijah and the prophets of Baal, Daniel and his friends and, uniquely, Jesus in the garden of Gethsemane. God never forsakes any of them.

Gideon's experience here is a story for our time, our generation. In many countries Christians are isolated, unable to live out their faith in public. Throughout the world, young Christians find their faith challenged in school.

> ... the LORD said ... 'I am going to give it [the Midianite camp] into your hands.'
>
> **Judges 7:9**

RESPOND

Pray that Christians you know of, isolated for their faith, may be confident of God's presence and power within them, for 'if God is for us, who can be against us?' (Romans 8:31).

Bible in a year: Mark 2; Psalm 89

Not a sword in sight

PREPARE

When were you last aware of trusting God to do something that mattered to you?

. . . .

READ

Judges 7:15–24

EXPLORE

Just imagine: it's around 10pm, one set of tired watchmen in the Midianite camp being replaced by another set who may be half-asleep and unfamiliar to those on the first watch. There is complete darkness when the silence is broken by the blast of trumpets, smashing pots, victory cries and lights burning around the camp! No wonder the Midianite army erupts into chaos, soldiers turning upon one another in panic, rushing to escape. Maybe some of the 20,000 Israelites who had been stood down, along with some from Ephraim, join Gideon's platoon in hot pursuit of the enemy – 'A sword for the Lord and for Gideon!' (v 20).

We might think that all Gideon and his troops had to do was to be bystanders. That would not be true. They had been called upon to follow Gideon and Gideon had to put his trust in God, actively cooperating with God.

Here's a question: in what ways do we intentionally communicate to others that God really can be trusted, and we actively live in the light of that? Younger generations, living in a world with opportunities, chaos, violence and godlessness, need to know this.

Trust in the Lord with all your heart and lean not on your own understanding.

Proverbs 3:5

RESPOND

Think of one person, place or situation where you long for what is wrong to be put right, only you cannot imagine how. With this in mind, reflect on Gideon's experience of actively cooperating with God, to achieve the impossible.

. . . .

Bible in a year: Mark 3; Colossians 1

Praise without limits

PREPARE
Imagine, are you coming into God's presence quickly or slowly, eagerly or reluctantly, alert or weary, distracted or focused?

READ
Psalm 148

EXPLORE
I'm writing this note in Holy Trinity Church, Blythburgh in Suffolk, known as the Cathedral in the Marshes. The angel roof in the fifteenth-century church is stunning. Originally brightly coloured, 11 angels remain, lifted high above the full length of the church, back-to-back, outstretched wings drawing the eyes of worshippers into God's presence. Sunlight streams down the chancel.

This psalm starts with the praise of angels in the highest heavens, shifts to the second heaven of sun and moon, then moves on to the heavens nearest us, the rain clouds. They all offer unending praise to God by their very existence – mainly without using words.

Then we reach the earth (vs 7–12). The genius of contemporary photography displays exquisite and unimaginable images of nature, calling forth praise and honour to God. Praising God tends to be described in terms of words, but the created world honours God by just being with its sheer biodiversity, by procreation, by seasonal transformation, by demonstration of awesome power. The psalm begins with mysterious angels who worship God in the heavens and deliver God's messages by words. It ends with children who communicate verbally but in many other ways.

> Let them praise the name of the LORD, for his name alone is exalted; his splendour is above the earth and the heavens.

Psalm 148:13

RESPOND
Pray that all generations gathering in God's presence today will be able to offer joy-filled, unfettered praise to the Lord whose splendour is above both earth and the heavens.

Bible in a year: Mark 4; Colossians 2

Waves of faithlessness

PREPARE
What do you long for God to do among your own family and friends?

••

READ
Judges 8:22–35

EXPLORE

God chose Gideon despite his flawed character. We may admire him because he refuses to be made a king. Or we may dislike him. After the defeat of the Midianites he behaves like a king, doling out violent punishment to anyone who crosses him. He even gives one of his sons the name 'Abimelek' which means 'my father is king'!

Similarly to Solomon, Gideon began well (v 23). Solomon built the Temple; Gideon destroyed a pagan altar. Both had many wives. Towards the end of their lives both encouraged the worship of false gods. Gideon, like Aaron who constructed the golden calf, created an idol out of gold donated from the spoil of his conquest (v 27). Ultimately, the worship of false gods is seen as the chief characteristic of the generation that followed Gideon (v 33). How could they forget the God of the covenant, the Holy God who had victoriously defeated the Midianites?

The story of God's people continues with its pattern of brief faithfulness to God followed by a lengthy pursuit of evil. Most accounts of outbreaks of spiritual revival, often inspired by a leader, are characterised by a collective recognition of sin, returning to a holy God. Leadership after Gideon was godless.

The LORD reigns, let the nations tremble…

Psalm 99:1

RESPOND

'You have rejected us, God … you have been angry – now restore us!' (Psalm 60:1). Pray boldly and imaginatively that future generations in both your family and in society will be characterised by Christlikeness.

••

Bible in a year: Mark 5; Psalm 90

Tuesday 13 August
Judges 13:1–25

Trust a woman!

PREPARE
Prepare to be amused and challenged by the first part of the Samson story. Ask God to meet with you, maybe in an unexpected way.

· ·

READ
Judges 13:1–25

EXPLORE
The book of Judges includes three outstanding women – Deborah, Jephthah's daughter (11:32–39) and Samson's mother. I grew up being told it was extraordinary that the first person to meet the resurrected Jesus was a woman: extraordinary because a woman's testimony was not valued. This was not Jesus' opinion. I was also aware of Hagar who felt so valued by God that she is the only person in the Hebrew Bible who gave God a name – 'the God who sees me' (Genesis 16:13)!

Here we have a woman whose husband, Manoah, does not trust his unnamed wife's testimony. But the angel of Lord insists it is she who's been entrusted with a message and a role from God (v 13). She is determined to take on the demanding task. Both of Samson's parents see the ascending flaming angel – though Manoah is slow to understand (v 21). His wife thinks more pragmatically (v 23).

Traditionally social hierarchies have limited the status of and opportunities for women. As a result, women appear less frequently in the Bible's narrative. But there are enough stories to demonstrate that both God the Father and God the Son value women counterculturally. This is an important truth to pass on to future generations.

'If the LORD had meant to kill us, he would not have ... shown us all these things.'
Judges 13:23

RESPOND
Thank God for the women you know who are faithfully communicating the good news of Jesus to younger generations.

· ·

Bible in a year: Mark 6; Colossians 3

Family faith passed on

PREPARE

How does it feel when you cannot understand what God is doing?

· ·

READ

Judges 14:1–20

EXPLORE

Children experience their parents' faith values from birth. Soon afterwards, parents begin to be challenged as their child's character, willpower and independence emerge. Samson's parents have a son who is both strong-willed and physically strong! As Samson was chosen by God before his conception, they abided by the Nazirite dietary regulations. They want him to marry within the Israelite community (v 3). Had they known the honey he shared with them had come from the carcass of a dead lion (v 9), forbidden by Jewish law, they'd have been appalled.

They could not know about the future (v 4), that God would use their son to separate the Israelites from the Philistines. As the Philistines 'rule' over Israel (v 4) the two nations currently appear to intermingle, evidence of Israel's compromising faithlessness to God. Yet, for all Samson's fury, the Spirit of the Lord comes upon him (vs 6,19). However poor his personal choices, he is still in the hands of God. His parents receive him back home after this dreadful escapade.

Christian parents have a God-given responsibility to pass on their faith to their children, by personal role-modelling, words and actions, and, like Samson's parents, have no idea of the future choices their child will make.

> His [Samson's] parents did not know that this was from the LORD…
>
> **Judges 14:4**

RESPOND

Pray for Christian parents you know as they seek to nurture their child's relationship with Christ, and pray for any parents whose child appears to have turned from Christ (for the time being).

· ·

Bible in a year: Mark 7; Colossians 4

What motivates leaders?

PREPARE
Reflect on those leaders in your own life who have influenced you for the glory of God.

....

READ
Judges 15:1–20

EXPLORE

History is scattered with national leaders whose personal ambitions far outweigh any desire to rule their people wisely. Our present age is no exception. An angel told Samson's mother her son would deliver Israel from the Philistines (13:5). He successfully fulfils that prophecy. Motivated by a desire for personal vengeance, in a fit of burning anger (v 3; 14:19), he kills a thousand Philistines and destroys their livelihood (vs 4,5,15). But there's little evidence he cares for his own people – a poor role model for future generations. He is unlike other judges who not only defeat Israel's enemies but also rule Israel in a period of peace.

Nonetheless, the Spirit of the Lord comes powerfully upon him to satisfy his desire for vengeance (v 14). He does cry out to God (v 18), albeit to meet his personal needs. The writer does not commend Samson as an example to follow but does acknowledge that God uses even the worst of leaders.

Jesus came to serve, ultimately giving his life as a ransom for many. By his actions and words, he demonstrated that 'whoever wants to become great among you must be your servant' (Mark 10:43,45). This is true leadership, a model he passed on to others, at great personal cost.

Samson led Israel for twenty years in the days of the Philistines.
Judges 15:20

RESPOND
Pray for those in authority over you in various contexts including Christian ones, and for those nations currently ruled by tyrants, recognising that the Spirit of the Lord remains ever-active.

....

Bible in a year: Mark 8; 1 Thessalonians 1

That famous haircut

PREPARE

This is a well-known story, probably the best known in Judges. Ask God to give you fresh insight today.

READ

Judges 16:1–22

EXPLORE

The people of Israel are still subjects of and influenced by the idol-worshipping Philistines. We don't know what sort of a judge Samson is but it's no surprise that there is little distinctively God-like about him in this penultimate chapter of his life. He remains free to move around Philistia, intermarrying and partying, confident of the secret source of his strength.

Yet he has plenty of reason to be afraid. Too many people hate him. Gradually he gets closer and closer to betraying his secret – the secret of his strength (v 6). Eventually, he tells Delilah everything. His head is shorn. His strength leaves him, but more strikingly, the Lord leaves him (v 20). His Nazirite vow is broken. No longer able to see (v 21), and thus not able to do whatever he fancies, as his own people have done (17:6; 21:25), he finally 'sees' what his life's faithful commitment to the vow represents –

God's calling and presence with him. It is almost too late.

Although Samson was grounded in the faith values of Israel, he'd not made them his own. Young people may hear fragments of the gospel of Christ but do not piece them together to make any sense. The gospel is not being passed on to them.

But the hair on his head began to grow again...

Judges 16:22

RESPOND

Pray that the Spirit of the Lord will fall powerfully on Scripture Union's mission to reach the estimated 95 per cent of young people not yet part of a Christian community.

Bible in a year: Mark 9; Psalm 91

Set apart for God

PREPARE

We've come full circle. Look back to the start of this series. God's covenant calls his people to be holy, set apart from other nations and worshipping him alone.

READ

Judges 16:23–31

EXPLORE

The Israelites are living among worshippers of the Philistine god Dagon, the god of agricultural prosperity. The capture of Samson, the Philistines' arch enemy, is attributed to him (v 23). (He is also mentioned in 1 Samuel 5 and 1 Chronicles 10.) God responds to Samson's desperate cry for strength (v 28), so that thousands of Philistines die with him as the temple of Dagon collapses, including 'all' the Philistine rulers. The lack of leaders may have served to weaken Philistine control over Israel. The God of Israel has proved to be the true Lord of all.

The book of Judges is a tale of God's people compromising in worship and lifestyle, with the occasional return in repentance to their Sovereign Lord. Community memory and religious practices are not sufficient to bind them to God. They are unable to remain faithful.

Pressures on Christians today to compromise are attractively strong. But we live in a different era. Christ has died, has risen and the Spirit has come. The apostle Paul writes: 'In view of God's mercy … offer your bodies as a living sacrifice, holy and pleasing to God – this is your true and proper worship' (Romans 12:1). It is possible to remain a 'holy, chosen people' because the Spirit is constantly with us.

Do not conform to the pattern of this world…

Romans 12:2

RESPOND

Pray that your words and actions will daily influence the next generation.

Bible in a year: Mark 10; 1 Thessalonians 2

Sing a new song!

PREPARE

'Strength will rise as we wait upon the Lord ... Our God, you reign for ever, our hope, our Strong Deliverer ... You're the defender of the weak, you comfort those in need. You lift us up on wings like eagles.'* Reflect on these lyrics.

READ

Psalm 149

EXPLORE

What one phrase from this psalm has struck you particularly? The instruction to sing a new song appears in Psalm 96 and Psalm 98. But here, faithful people, covered by God's covenant love, are urged three times to sing such a song of praise (vs 1,3,5). Maybe joy robs people of sleep, or maybe sleep is possible, knowing the joy of safekeeping (v 5).

The ancient people of Israel frequently faced life-threatening dangers. But what are we to make of the unexpected intrusion of the warlike language in verses 6–9? Maybe the key lies in the 'double-edged sword' (v 6). Today God's faithful people are endangered, though our struggle is not primarily against flesh and blood (Ephesians 6:12). So, with one edge, we hold on to the sword of the Spirit which is the word of God as we engage in battle (Ephesians 6:17); with the other, we access the joy found in praise at the start of this psalm, knowing God is the Maker of the whole world and reigns as everlasting King (v 2). This is not a tension, but a living reality.

Sing to the LORD a new song, his praise in the assembly of his faithful people.

Psalm 149:1

RESPOND

Allow yourself to rejoice that the Lord takes delight in you (v 4). If possible, sing or listen to a recording of the song 'Strength Will Rise' as you wait upon the Lord.

*'Strength Will Rise', Brenton Brown, Ken Riley, Thankyou Music/PRS, © 2005

Bible in a year: Mark 11; 1 Thessalonians 3

Messy but miraculous

Working with the church in Corinth was no cakewalk. But is any church entirely devoid of petty jealousies, competing views and conflicting personalities? Paul followed Augustine's dictum when he spoke about Christians who wilted under persecution: 'We must never despair about anyone at all.'* Paul seeks patiently to heal divides and correct wrong thinking within his overriding vision of a unified church, with love at its core.

About the writer
Andy Bathgate

Andy retired as CEO of SU Scotland in 2020 after 19 years. In retirement, he filled his time volunteering with Edinburgh City Mission and leadership in his local church, amongst other things. Shortly after writing these notes, Andy went to be with his Saviour in heaven.

*Quoted in B Myers, *The Apostles' Creed*, Lexham Press, 2018, p115

He tackles potential disruption in worship by treading a careful path between a full expression of the gifts of the Spirit and maintaining an order that enables the church to be strengthened. He wants people to be free to use their gifts but always in a context where these gifts nurture faith and unity, reflecting the God of order. He understands how gifts can be abused, drawing attention to ourselves and dominating others.

Then he has some muddled thinking about resurrection to straighten out. You might think they would have grasped this already. However, the detail in which Paul speaks shows that their experience of the Spirit was way ahead of their understanding of the truth. And we too benefit from understanding the resurrection as much more than an adjunct to the cross. It is core to Christian truth and right living.

He draws to a close by encouraging generosity of spirit both financially and in hospitality. We finish on Sunday with Psalm 150, a perfect example of the corporate, unified worship which would gladden Paul's heart.

Gifted for growth

PREPARE

Give thanks that in the church God has provided us with 'everything we need for a godly life' (2 Peter 1:3).

READ

1 Corinthians 14:1–25

EXPLORE

Sometimes we place greater emphasis on personal time with God than on our corporate worship. Both are important but Paul focuses here on the benefits of sharing in the gifts and insights of others. He is consumed by the need for Christians to grow in faith and unity. That happens best when spiritual gifts are used to nurture one another, by speaking intelligible words of truth to each other.

So, speaking in tongues (possibly ordinary foreign languages or angelic speech; see 13:1) is excellent for individual worship but may not be edifying for others (v 17) – unless of course the unknown languages are interpreted. Prophecy is more beneficial because it speaks in a known language and strengthens, encourages and comforts (v 3). It's not all about me. So let's long for gifts that build the community.

God used foreign tongues in the past as a sign of judgement to Israel (eg Isaiah 28:11–13). They had not listened to his voice and incomprehensible tongues confirmed them in their sin. If people hear but do not understand they cannot repent. They are left bemused (v 23). But prophecy leaves people in no doubt about their need. Getting behind their defences, it can fulfil our longing that they recognise God's presence.

Since you are eager for gifts of the Spirit, try to excel in those that build up the church.

1 Corinthians 14:12

RESPOND

What gift has God given you that can grow others in faith and unity? Are there fresh opportunities you can discern to use your gift more effectively?

Bible in a year: Mark 12; Psalms 92,93

Organised spontaneity

PREPARE

Meditate on the greatness of the God who brought order to chaos at creation and who brings harmony between disparate people in salvation.

READ

1 Corinthians 14:26–40

EXPLORE

'Rammy' is a word used in Scotland for a quarrel or disorder. There's increased potential for a rammy in a church gathering where different people choose hymns, bring instruction or a revelation with others speaking in interpreted tongues and prophesying! But 'vibrancy and order are not enemies'* if our agreed criterion is building up the church (v 26). It's not a competition! Where our common motivation is instruction and encouragement (v 31) and when prophets control themselves (v 32), then even interruption is tolerated (v 30). It's an image which challenges protective practices when it comes to worship-leading and preaching! A prophet can kindly give way to another with a revelation, choosing not to hog the limelight but allowing other contributions. Space is provided for all God's people to bring their insights. It looks as if prophecy is not a prepared talk, but neither is it an uncontested word from the Lord (v 29).

We can only guess that some wives were prone to air their questions about prophecies, challenging their husbands in public, which was far from the done thing (vs 34,35)! Given 1 Corinthians 11:5, it is clearly not a lifetime ban! Rather, this restriction aims to nullify distraction from building up the church (v 26).

When you come together … Everything must be done so that the church may be built up.

1 Corinthians 14:26

RESPOND

Examine your own heart to question your motives for speaking and how well you listen to others.

*TR Schreiner, *1 Corinthians*, IVP, 2018, p295

Bible in a year: Mark 13; 1 Thessalonians 4

Don't budge

PREPARE
'On Christ the solid rock I stand.'* Come again to reaffirm your faith in him.

∙∙∙

READ
1 Corinthians 15:1–11

EXPLORE
Despite tensions in Corinth, something held them together. They had all heard and gladly received the good news about Jesus. They now stood together on that solid ground. Like them, remaining loyal to that commitment is critical for us because 'final salvation will not come without perseverance'.** As Jesus taught us, sprouting seeds may have inadequate roots or life choked out of them (Matthew 13:20–22).

Can you sum up the gospel in one word? 'Jesus' is Scott McKnight's answer.*** Sometimes it's made primarily about us and our needs! Jesus is the fulfilment of all God's plans. He really died and was buried to confirm it. He rose again and his appearance to numerous people validated it. His death accomplishes something that had plagued humanity since creation: the separation sin causes between humans and God. Jesus' resurrection proclaims that sin and death could not hold him (Acts 2:24). Far from simply passing on a story, Paul is personally wrapped up in this. To his immense surprise, Jesus chose to appear to him (v 8). Personal testimony has its place; the reality of Jesus 'appearing' to *us*. But of first importance is centring people's attention on Jesus, his death and resurrection. This is a life-giving story which draws people to give themselves unremittingly for Jesus.

> By this gospel you are saved, if you hold firmly to the word I preached to you …
>
> **1 Corinthians 15:2**

RESPOND
What's so good about the good news of Jesus' death and resurrection? Why do you think so many don't think it's good news? Can we change that?

*'My hope is built', Edward Mote, 1834 **TR Schreiner, *1 Corinthians*, IVP, 2018, p301
***S McKnight, 'The One Word Gospel', *Substack* blog, 3 July 2023

∙∙∙

Bible in a year: Mark 14; 1 Thessalonians 5

Death is not the end

PREPARE
'Jesus lives! The victory won / Death no longer can appal me.'* Give thanks that the living Lord is with you now.

READ
1 Corinthians 15:12–34

EXPLORE
An atheist headteacher welcomed Scripture Union into his school because of its moral benefits. Like him, others want Jesus without the supernatural. Some in Corinth were attracted to Jesus but not the idea of resurrection. Dead people at best continued as spirits, lesser versions of themselves – but bodily resurrected? Core to Christian belief is the resurrection of Jesus and the promise that holds for those who belong to him. Taken to its logical conclusion, there is no Christian faith without it. Faith becomes a husk, empty and futile (vs 17,18). It's pitiful. Those who have died stay dead. No one escapes being mired in sin. As for the apostles, no resurrection makes them snake-oil salesmen (vs 29–32). Their efforts are a waste of time and energy. It all hangs on the resurrection.

Jesus has been raised, countering all that Adam spoiled. Adam's legacy is death. Jesus bequeaths life. He is raised and all those *in Christ* rise with him into new life and on the final day share Jesus' indestructible life (v 22). Every threat is removed, every enemy neutered. One of us, a real human being, accomplishes this for us. Then the human Jesus presents his victory to his Father, and God is truly honoured (v 28).

> But Christ has indeed been raised from the dead, the firstfruits of those who have fallen asleep.
>
> **1 Corinthians 15:20**

RESPOND
Reflect on all that comes to you through the resurrection. Allow your day to be shaped by that, even if people are 'beastly' to you (v 32).

*From the hymn 'Jesus Lives!' by Christian Gellert (1715–1769)

Bible in a year: Mark 15; 2 Thessalonians 1

What's in store?

PREPARE
Pray: 'Dear Lord, may I realise afresh today what your death and resurrection mean for me. Amen.'

....

READ
1 Corinthians 15:35–58

EXPLORE

The Nobel Prize-winning writer, Elias Canetti, 'rejected death',* but we don't know exactly how he planned to implement this rejection! We are compelled to acknowledge our limitations in this regard as perishable (sell-by date withheld), weak, earthly and mortal (vs 42–54). But Christians do live in defiance of death. It doesn't have the final word over our frail bodies. We are 'Swimming in a sea of sorrow / Heading for a world of promise'.** A promise founded on the victory of the Lord Jesus Christ.

Paul's writing is contrast-laden. Human bodies contrast with other bodies both in the heavens and on earth. Even in their present perishable form they carry a degree of splendour (v 40). They are God-given and therefore have a beauty and value. But they are not God's final masterpiece. If he can create all these splendid bodies, then he is quite capable of producing something even more magnificent. No longer tied to our family lineage in Adam, we share in the victory of Jesus; that signals transformation, tackling every previous limitation (vs 52–54). In Jesus we do 'reject death'. That's not 'pie in the sky when you die'. It transforms life here, giving stability and value to all we do (v 58).

> But thanks be to God! He gives us the victory through our Lord Jesus Christ.
>
> **1 Corinthians 15:57**

RESPOND
Is there some work you have done for the Lord as a Christian that you feel was a failure? Is that the best way to think of it in the light of future resurrection?

*Quoted in D Athill, *Somewhere Towards the End*, Granta, 2009, p6
**'Sea of Sorrow' by Belle and Sebastian, 2022. Words and Music, a division of Big Deal Music LLC

....

Bible in a year: Mark 16; Psalm 94

Saturday 24 August
1 Corinthians 16:1–24

God's curators

PREPARE
'The grace of the Lord Jesus be with you' (16:23). Use this phrase to reflect on God's work in your life.

READ
1 Corinthians 16:1–24

EXPLORE

Having traversed the soaring heights of the coming of Christ and final resurrection, Paul now talks money! He transitions to practicalities: gathering up a collection; organising future visits. John Wesley, when asked what he would do if this was his last day on earth, supposedly read out his appointments' diary. Paul likewise sees no conflict between high theology and the day-to-day. It's not unspiritual hassle; it's how Christian people do life.

There are needs to be met demanding planning not just prayer! Our finances require planning with measures put in place to ensure their proper handling (vs 2–4). But money isn't Paul's priority. He's a people person with a heart for the needy in Jerusalem (v 3) and for his troublesome friends in Corinth. He's not interested in ticking a box through a fleeting visit. He wants to give them quality time (v 7). He's protective of

Timothy (v 11) and, although there's tension in the relationship with Apollos, he's still 'our brother' (v 12). Relationships are vital. And it's not all one way. The phrase 'they refreshed my spirit' (v 18) reveals Paul's needs. He is passionate for people, but even more for Jesus. The startling condemnation on those who do not 'love the Lord' (v 22) says a great deal about his feelings when Jesus is not honoured as Lord.

> Be on your guard; stand firm in the faith; be courageous; be strong. Do everything in love.
>
> **1 Corinthians 16:13,14**

RESPOND
What can you learn from Paul's practical theology? Whose spirit could you refresh today?

Bible in a year: Ecclesiastes 1–3; 2 Thessalonians 2

Loud and proud

PREPARE
Praise the Lord by singing a favourite song, getting on your knees to pray, clapping your hands or playing a musical instrument for him.

READ
Psalm 150

EXPLORE
Psalm 150 leaves us in no doubt what we are required to do: 'Praise the LORD'. Whoever you are, wherever you are, whatever instrument you play, the top priority is acknowledging God and giving him thanks. If you have any breath in your body, if you are a human living on earth or a being in his 'mighty heavens' (v 1 – possibly angelic beings), praise the Lord and, to be frank, let it rip! If you can't play an instrument (wind, string and percussion are available), you can always dance (v 4).

Exuberant praise is worthy of the God who acts in salvation for helpless humans. These instruments are mostly difficult to play softly. This praise just can't be done in a quiet corner. Everybody needs to hear and know about this God. This doesn't negate the worth of quiet and contemplative worship. But there are times to break out; forgetting about what others think; working against any cultural inhibitions and making it known how much we adore this God. He is the God who reciprocates this praise by singing over his people. Zephaniah 3:17 pictures the Lord singing over his people with either 'joyful' (NLT) or even 'loud' (RSV) songs. He loves us that much.

Let everything that has breath praise the LORD.
Psalm 150:6

RESPOND
This is corporate worship on a grand scale. Are there people outside your usual group that you could join together with to praise the Lord?

Bible in a year: Ecclesiastes 4,5; 2 Thessalonians 3

The golden thread

It was Old Testament Israel's unique calling to be God's own nation, fleshing out God's character in their everyday lives. As they did so, the onlooking nations could understand the beauty of God, translated into the workings of Israel's culture. The trouble is that Israel, time and again, failed to fulfil this calling. God's response was to send prophets to remind them of their God-given identity and warn of the consequences of ignoring their vocation.

Micah was one such prophet: an ordinary man (possibly a farmer) charged with the passion and words of God. His ministry was exercised in the eighth century BC, during a time of dramatic international upheaval. Israel itself was enjoying a time of prosperity, but at a high social cost. The prosperous were gaining wealth at the expense of the poor (6:10–12). An increasingly secular culture (albeit with a veneer of religious respectability, 3:11) was replacing a God-honouring society in which the poor, the widow, the orphan and the foreigner should have been duly cared for (Deuteronomy 14:28,29).

The threat of the invading Assyrians was not just a symptom of global power shifts: it was a direct result of Israel turning away from God (1:5).

And yet, even as Micah delivers God's confrontative and warning messages to Israel, judgement is never his last word. Micah's 'sermons' are shot through with hope, rooted in the eternal purposes of a faithful and unchanging God.

About the writer
David Lawrence

David is currently the Teaching Pastor at Thornbury Baptist Church, near Bristol. In the past he has worked with Scripture Union, ForMission (Springdale College), the Methodist Church of Great Britain and the London Institute for Contemporary Christianity.

No soft touch

PREPARE
Jesus said, 'If you love me, keep my commands' (John 14:15). How has your love for Jesus resulted in changes in your behaviour?

READ
Micah 1:1 – 2:5

EXPLORE
Israel knew that God was 'compassionate and gracious … slow to anger, abounding in love and faithfulness', but they were on track for learning that he also cares deeply about sin, and that 'he does not leave the guilty unpunished' (Exodus 34:7). It was Micah's painful job (v 8) to warn both north and south Israel (Samaria and Judah) that their wilful defiance was about to bring God's judgement on them (v 5).

They had broken their covenant with God, and there was a price to pay. The first two commandments (Exodus 20:3–6) had been forsaken in Samaria (vs 6,7), and the contagion had spread to Jerusalem (v 9). As sin took root in Jerusalem a host of other commandments were disregarded. Theft, coveting and fraud became legitimised modes of doing business, and inevitably it was the poor that suffered (2:1,2).

God is no soft touch and will not tolerate sin within his people for ever. In both Old and New Testaments, continued rebellion will earn the consequences of divine displeasure (eg Revelation 2:4,5,14–16,20–23).

> All this is because of Jacob's transgression, because of the sins of the people of Israel.
> **Micah 1:5**

RESPOND
Sit with these words from Psalm 139:23,24. What might God wish to say to you?
'Search me, God, and know my heart; test me and know my anxious thoughts. See if there is any offensive way in me, and lead me in the way everlasting.'

Bible in a year: Ecclesiastes 6,7; Psalms 95,96

Tuesday 27 August
Micah 2:6 – 3:12

None so deaf

PREPARE

When did you last hear God speaking to you through another person? What did he say and how did you respond?

READ
Micah 2:6 – 3:12

EXPLORE

Micah found it hard to get a hearing because there were so many other prophets who were saying the exact opposite of his message. 'Don't listen to Micah,' they said. 'He's got God all wrong' (v 6). 'God would never judge *us – we* are *his people!*' (v 7).

Telling people what they want to hear makes you popular (2:11) and even wealthy (3:11) but does not guarantee that what you are saying is right. Those who claim to speak in the name of God can, in fact, be leading people astray (3:5). So how to tell the difference between the true and the false prophets? True prophets, like Micah, are not interested in popularity or wealth, but their message – and their lives – resonate with God's justice and his holiness (3:8). Their message will often challenge culture and call people back to God's truth (3:1), yet always with a strong injection of hope (2:12,13).

Choosing to listen to people who say just what we want to hear is a constant temptation (2 Timothy 4:3). But there are none so deaf as those who will not hear.

> If a liar and deceiver comes and says, 'I will prophesy for you plenty of wine and beer,' that would be just the prophet for this people!
> **Micah 2:11**

RESPOND

Pray for those you know whose work is to preach and teach God's Word. Pray that they hear God clearly, and boldly deliver what God has given to them. Consider thanking them for faithfully bringing God's Word to you.

Bible in a year: Ecclesiastes 8,9; 1 Timothy 1

The golden thread

PREPARE

Prayerfully repeat these words from Psalm 16:5 (GNT): 'You, Lord, are all I have, and you give me all I need; my future is in your hands.' As you pray, listen for what God may wish to say to you.

READ

Micah 4:1–13

EXPLORE

There's no escaping it, Israel's rebellion is going to be the cause of great pain for the nation and for the individuals that comprise it (v 10). Writhing in agony at their loss, they will watch Babylon take away everything they value, then destroy the rest (v 11).

In times of great suffering and loss it can be hard to hang on to any sense of God's presence or purpose. 'Where is God in this mess?' we wonder. Perhaps that is why in this passage, the word that comes more often than any other is 'the Lord'. Despite everything, he is still the central character in the unfolding events.

Ten times (vs 1,2,2,4,5,6,7,10,12,13) Micah threads the name of 'the Lord' through this passage, as an active participant in everything that is going on. Wonderfully, justice, peace, contentment and freedom from fear are on his agenda (vs 3,4)! God

may permit us to suffer the consequences of our own choices (1:5), but the golden thread, woven through even our most difficult times, is the faithful presence of 'the Lord'.

> 'In that day,' declares the Lord, 'I will gather the lame; I will assemble the exiles and those I have brought to grief.'
>
> **Micah 4:6**

RESPOND

Bring the events of the world to mind and pray for the day when 'nation will not take up sword against nation' any more (v 3). Pray for Christians caught in conflict to find hope and sanctuary in the Lord.

Bible in a year: Ecclesiastes 10,11; 1 Timothy 2

Small people: big difference

PREPARE

Have you ever been in a situation where it was hard being in a minority as a Christian? How did it feel and how did you respond? Looking back, how might you have responded differently?

. . . .

READ

Micah 5:1–15

EXPLORE

Did you make it through the reading without singing 'O Little Town of Bethlehem'?

The suffering of Israel would not be resolved by human ingenuity, nor their enemies overthrown by violent rebellion. Rather, Micah prophesies that God himself will intervene to establish a new leader, to be born in an obscure little town near Jerusalem (v 2). This strong, majestic and godly leader (v 4) will finally become the nation's peace (v 5). The people he leads will be a minority (remnant), and it is therefore perhaps surprising that their purified lives (vs 10–14) will have a positive effect on the world. Living in 'the midst of many peoples' they will be a refreshing presence (v 7), and a tenacious force for God's truth (v 8).

As Christians today, in the minority in our countries, it's easy to become defensive or to pull up the drawbridge against a hostile culture. But the people of God's King from Bethlehem have a mandate to be a force for good wherever they are and whatever they do.

> The remnant of Jacob will be in the midst of many peoples like dew from the LORD, like showers on the grass, which do not … depend on man.
>
> **Micah 5:7**

RESPOND

Think of one situation where you can make a difference this week by being a source of God's refreshment, or a courageous bearer of God's truth. Pray for that situation and your role there now.

. . . .

Bible in a year: Ecclesiastes 12; 1 Timothy 3

Walking partner

PREPARE

'There is no place where earth's sorrows / Are more felt than up in Heaven; / There is no place where earth's failings / Have such kindly judgment given.'* Take your sorrows and failings to the place of tender mercy.

READ

Micah 6:1–16

EXPLORE

Israel are in the dock and God is making his accusations (v 2). Despite all his kindness to them (vs 4,5), they have rejected him, walking away after other gods (v 16).

So, how to put things right with God? One response Micah considers is to make impossible religious commitments (vs 6,7). Perhaps today we are not tempted to offer thousands of rams! But maybe we resolve to pray harder; never miss church; give more than a tithe; read the Bible in a year. All good things, but not the heart of our relationship with God.

Israel had to learn that the good life God requires is not 'right religion' but 'right relationships' with God and others. Never mind the year-old calves (v 6); start showing mercy to those who offend you, and act justly in your dealings with others (v 8). Easier said than done,

and such a generous life can only be resourced by humbly walking with God. Only time spent in God's presence can shape us into God's people.

He has shown you, O mortal, what is good. And what does the Lord require of you? To act justly and to love mercy and to walk humbly with your God.

Micah 6:8

RESPOND

What does it mean for you, to 'walk humbly with your God'? How does walking with him affect your relationships, at home, at work, with friends? Why not literally go out for a walk with God and talk it through with him?

*Frederick W Faber, 1854

Bible in a year: Song of Songs 1,2; Psalms 97,98

Joyful mercy

PREPARE

Use this simple prayer as you come to God. You may like to repeat it a few times: 'Jesus, lead me to the Father's embrace. Father, fill me with your Holy Spirit. Spirit, empower me to live for Jesus.'

READ
Micah 7:1–20

EXPLORE

Is there an activity you particularly enjoy: something that in a stressful week makes you feel happy? God has something like that: he 'delights to show mercy' (v 18)!

Forgiving those who have wronged him (v 18) lights up his week (so to speak!). Re-engaging with his estranged people thrills him to his core! No grudging acceptance of outcasts, but, like the father in the prodigal son story told by Jesus, a joyful, arms-open-wide, let's-throw-a-party kind of renewal.

Israel, to be sure, were still a long way from enjoying this divine embrace. Their lives were in disorder (vs 2–6) and they would still suffer for their actions (v 9). But Micah knew that rebellion and judgement would not be the last words over Israel. His eye wasn't so much on the disorder, as on his God (v 7). His hope was in the unchangeable nature of God's character (v 18), and the unshakeable reliability of God's promises (v 20). When all seems broken and lost, don't despair. Keep looking to the God who *delights* to show mercy (v 18).

You do not stay angry for ever but delight to show mercy.

Micah 7:18

RESPOND

It's been said that justice is giving people what they deserve, but mercy is giving them far more than they deserve. Is there anyone to whom you need to show mercy? How might you go about that this week?

Bible in a year: Song of Songs 3,4; 1 Timothy 4

How to be happy

PREPARE

'Tell God all that is in your heart' (François Fénelon, 1651–1715). **The psalms give us permission to bring ourselves, 'warts and all', to God in prayer. Take a moment to pour out your heart's contents to God.**

READ

Psalm 1

EXPLORE

A wise man once wrote that if you want to be happy, don't pursue happiness: rather, stop doing the things that make you unhappy! This psalm starts with the word 'blessed', which has the meaning of 'happy'. 'Happy is the one who stops doing the things that lead to unhappiness!' (vs 1–3).

Keeping in step with, or standing in line with, the values of a secular culture (v 1) is not the route to happiness, it seems. Rather, happiness is found in a life ordered by God's wisdom, as revealed in the Bible (v 2). God's Word needs to be given a high priority in the life of the one seeking true happiness (v 2). It's easy to fall in step with the world: it takes discipline to stay rooted in God.

The psalm offers a contrast between the impermanence of cultural fads ('the way that sinners take', v 1), and the enduring value of God's Word. The former, like chaff, is likely to disappear when the next wind of change blows through (v 4): the latter is permanently and powerfully potent (vs 3,6)!

> Blessed is the one who does not walk in step with the wicked or stand in the way that sinners take or sit in the company of mockers, but whose delight is in the law of the LORD…

Psalm 1:1,2

RESPOND

Where are you seeking happiness? Are there ways in which you've bought into contemporary culture's quest for happiness?

Bible in a year: Song of Songs 5,6; 1 Timothy 5

A hero unlike any other

About the writer
Richard Ellwood

After several years pastoring an international French-speaking church in Brussels, Belgium, Richard is now the Team Leader of the Salt & Light Advance family of churches. He lives with his wife and family in Oxfordshire.

Our cinemas are often dominated by action hero films. Whether it's Spider-Man swinging from buildings, the X-Men saving the universe or Indiana Jones battling to find lost historical artefacts, we have no shortage of this kind of film. We all love a hero and we probably all have assumptions about what a hero should be like: strong, athletic, brave, fast, sophisticated...

The 'hero' of John's Gospel is, of course, Jesus. He is, however, a hero entirely different from any we might see at the movies. In the chapters we shall be reading over the coming days, we see a hero who heals the sick, teaches profoundly about his identity, raises a man from the dead, weeps with his mourning family and is anointed with perfume before a dramatic yet humble entry into the great city of Jerusalem.

As you read these stories, look out for the portrayal of the hero at the heart of it all. Jesus is shown to be kind with those who are suffering and yet firm with those who are plotting against him. He's a man who performs extraordinary miracles, yet rides on the back of a donkey and speaks of being a 'shepherd' who 'lays down his life for the sheep' (John 10:11). John shows him as the master of events and yet full of humility. In reading these stories, wonder afresh at the true superhero of the world.

Monday 2 September
John 9:1–12

Clear vision

PREPARE
As you begin a new set of readings, ask the Holy Spirit to bring God's Word to life.

. . . .

READ
John 9:1–12

EXPLORE

How's your eyesight? Do you find it hard to read a book without squinting or reaching for your glasses? The ability to see easily is something not to be taken for granted. John 9 – which we will read over the next three days – is all about seeing clearly. The chapter centres on an intriguing story of a man born blind who has his sight miraculously healed by Jesus. This physical blindness is accompanied by spiritual blindness as the man has his spiritual eyes opened to who Jesus is while the watching Pharisees remain stubbornly blind (v 40).

There is a certain blindness among the crowd too as those watching are unsure if the blind man really is who they think. Is he the blind man they used to see begging? 'No, he only looks like him' (v 9). Then when asked where Jesus is, the healed man can't see Jesus anywhere (v 12). There is both physical and spiritual lack of vision everywhere.

And yet amid this stands Jesus who boldly states: 'I am the light of the world' (v 5). The man is blind, his world is naturally dark, and yet one encounter with Jesus, 'the light of the world', and his physical and spiritual sight are transformed.

'While I am in the world, I am the light of the world.'
John 9:5

RESPOND
Take a moment today to acknowledge Jesus as 'the light of the world'. Invite him to bring fresh light and revelation into your life.

. . . .

Bible in a year: Song of Songs 7,8; Psalms 99–101

Blind spots

PREPARE
How would you have responded to the miracle of the blind man?

. . . .

READ
John 9:13–34

EXPLORE
Learning to drive can be scary. Changing gears smoothly, mastering parallel parking, checking your mirrors regularly – there's so much to get used to! One key principle learner-drivers have to grasp quickly is that of blind spots. These are areas which you, as the driver, cannot see clearly. As the Pharisees learn of the miraculous healing of the blind man, they cannot see the wonder of what has happened due to their 'blind spots'. They are shocked that such a thing could have happened on a Sabbath and so immediately refuse to accept the validity of the miracle (v 16).

We can all have blind spots in our own lives – things we cannot 'see' because of prejudices, expectations or our own pride. The Pharisees miss out on the extraordinary privilege of knowing Jesus, the Son of God, because of their own blind spots. They couldn't see that Jesus had come to bring in a new era and usher in God's kingdom in a fresh way. It may seem absurd to us now that Jesus shouldn't heal people on certain days of the week, but for the Pharisees this was a key component of Jewish life. There's a challenge to us not to be like the Pharisees and miss what Jesus is doing in and around us because of preconceived ideas of how Jesus must work.

'If this man were not from God, he could do nothing.'
John 9:33

RESPOND
Ask God to highlight blind spots in your life where expectations and experiences are affecting how you see things.

. . . .

Bible in a year: Isaiah 1,2; 1 Timothy 6

A life turned around

PREPARE

What words sum up your walk with Jesus during this current season of your life?

· ·

READ

John 9:35–41

EXPLORE

Arriving at a destination after a long journey is a great feeling – relief that the journey is over and joy at all the destination brings. Today we read the final part of the journey of the man born blind. We have seen him go from physical blindness to seeing clearly and now his journey from spiritual blindness to spiritual sight is complete. This spiritual vision is again contrasted by John with the spiritual blindness of the Pharisees who remain blind to what is happening and who Jesus really is.

There is a wonderful simplicity to the journey of this man. It starts with struggle and pain before meeting Jesus. His encounter with Jesus is unusual as he has mud and saliva rubbed into his eyes! At the heart of the encounter, however, is one of the most precious characteristics of any disciple of Jesus – obedience, as the man follows the words of Jesus and washes in the Pool of Siloam (v 7). He then boldly defends the one who has healed him in his confrontation with the Pharisees (vs 30–33) before his personal moment with Jesus where he expresses his belief in him, and a life of worship begins (v 38). Obedience, boldness and worship – three essential elements to the life of any disciple of Jesus.

> Then the man said, 'Lord, I believe,' and he worshipped him.
>
> **John 9:38**

RESPOND

Take a moment to reflect on these three aspects of discipleship and ask Jesus if he is encouraging you to grow in any one of these.

· ·

Bible in a year: Isaiah 3–5; 2 Timothy 1

The sheep and the gate

PREPARE
Why do you think Jesus used the image of sheep to describe his followers?

READ
John 10:1–10

EXPLORE
To us today, a gate is an ordinary, uninspiring object. It is important but functional rather than exciting. Sheep, meanwhile, are not animals many of us have to deal with on a daily basis. We pass them in fields, see them in farms – we may even eat them from our plates. For Jesus' listeners in the agricultural society of first-century Israel, sheep were a key source of income for many families. And a gate in front of a sheep pen offered essential safety and protection. Jesus adopts this metaphor for himself, claiming to be a spiritual gate for any 'sheep' who choose to follow him.

Jesus then takes his illustration further, saying that he offers not only safety but also freedom and enjoyment. Anyone who enters through him 'will come in and go out, and find pasture' (v 9). This gate is not a restrictive, freedom-killing one; rather it is one which provides joy and life 'to the full' (v 10). By living according to the ways of Jesus the gate, we find two seeming opposites available to us: safety and protection but also liberty and pleasure.

Jesus is our gate, keeping us safe from the threats of the enemy but also offering freedom and satisfaction. This is how the Christian life is meant to be lived – balancing protection with freedom, safety with expansion and obedience with joy.

'Very truly I tell you, I am the gate for the sheep.'
John 10:7

RESPOND
Is your relationship with Jesus, 'the gate', characterised by these elements?

Bible in a year: Isaiah 6,7; 2 Timothy 2

Friday 6 September
John 10:11–21

The sheep and the shepherd

PREPARE

What difference does the fact Jesus is our 'good shepherd' make to your life?

READ
John 10:11–21

EXPLORE

Jesus is the 'gate' offering protection and freedom and the chance to live life 'to the full' (v 10). However, it doesn't stop there! In Jesus' time the roles of shepherd and gate were often blurred. The shepherd would double-up as the gate, often sleeping across the entrance of the sheep pen. In the same way, Jesus adopts both roles: gate and shepherd.

While gates and sheep are at least familiar parts of modern life, for most of us, shepherds are not. A shepherd may conjure images of long beards, long staffs and long days in the fields, but Jesus takes an everyday job of his time and applies it to himself, giving a clear promise to his followers.

Jesus says there is a key difference between him and the 'hired hands' (v 12) who may be placed in charge. Such men are not authentic in their care, leaving at the first sign of danger. Jesus, on the other hand, 'lays down his life for the sheep' (v 11), and gives a profound promise of intimacy and closeness to his followers. This shepherd really cares for his sheep. Just as sheep recognise the specific voice of their shepherd (vs 16,27), so can the followers of Jesus hear and recognise his voice. We too may 'know' (v 14) the good shepherd. What a promise!

> 'I am the good shepherd. The good shepherd lays down his life for the sheep.'
>
> **John 10:11**

RESPOND
Spend time today listening to the voice of the 'good shepherd' and thanking him afresh for his wonderful care for you.

Bible in a year: Isaiah 8,9; Psalm 102

The voice of the shepherd

PREPARE
Listen to the voice of the shepherd as you reflect on today's reading.

· ·

READ
John 10:22–42

EXPLORE
Every day we are bombarded with dubious promises and suspicious guarantees. It might be the latest must-have offer from our favourite streaming service or our insurance company offering us a supposedly unique deal for a 'limited period only'. These promises come and go, often accompanied by the all-important small print. They are not always as they seem.

In today's reading, Jesus finds himself in the heart of the Jerusalem Temple being quizzed once again by his opponents. In this hostile environment Jesus announces a wonderful promise: a genuinely unique, never-bettered, once-in-a-lifetime offer to all who accept it. To his 'sheep', Jesus says, 'I give them eternal life' (v 28). To those who listen to and obey the voice of Jesus, who choose to follow and live for Jesus, the promise of knowing him eternally is made.

As Jesus continues, it seems he anticipates the inevitable doubts that might creep into our minds at such a wonderful promise: 'Surely this is too good to be true. Surely I'm not good enough or Jesus will change his mind when I next mess up.' To these doubts, Jesus twice says that 'no one will snatch them out of my hand' (vs 28,29). This is a promise that's here to stay with no fine print!

> 'My sheep listen to my voice; I know them, and they follow me.'
> **John 10:27**

RESPOND
Do you doubt this promise of eternal life? Take time to reflect on this promise, asking God to bring assurance to your heart.

· ·

Bible in a year: Isaiah 10–12; 2 Timothy 3

Sunday 8 September
Psalm 3

God who sustains us

PREPARE
What is your natural response when the trials of life seem to mount up one upon the other?

READ
Psalm 3

EXPLORE
The great King David experienced his fair share of struggles in his life: bullying from his brothers, attempts on his life from King Saul, the death of some of his children and betrayal from his sons to name just some. It is this last wound which is the painful context for Psalm 3 – the jealousy and greed of his son Absalom which led him to try to take his father's throne (see 2 Samuel 13–19).

The context may be traumatic, but David, in all this pain, is able to lift his eyes to the Lord and see God's profound care. To him, God is a 'shield' and the one who 'lifts' him up (v 3). He is a personal God who not only hears the prayers of the king but 'answers' them too (v 4). This personal care extends to giving him the breath he needs to live each day. If David wakes each morning it is 'because the Lord sustains me' (v 5). David sees that although he may be the king of God's chosen people, he is still reliant on God for every breath that leaves his lungs. He is sustained by God during struggle and challenge, joy and delight.

> I lie down and sleep; I wake again, because the Lord sustains me.
>
> **Psalm 3:5**

RESPOND:
No matter the season of life you are currently in, thank God for his personal care over you today and that he is the one who 'sustains' you.

Bible in a year: Isaiah 13,14; 2 Timothy 4

Confusion reigns!

PREPARE

What is your natural response when things in life are unclear? To panic, to prepare or to pray?

READ

John 11:1–16

EXPLORE

The boring commute to work. The moody teenager. The close friend dying of cancer. From the mundane to the deeply painful, life can be full of things which bemuse, frustrate and hurt. Today we come to the opening of one of the most moving chapters of the New Testament. We may know how the story ends, but in its opening today there is one dominant emotion: confusion.

Jesus' actions are, at least at first sight, a little confusing. John tells us of Jesus' love and affection for Lazarus and his sisters yet, despite this, 'when [Jesus] heard that Lazarus was ill, he stayed where he was two more days' (v 6). Confusion is clearly felt by the disciples too as they question why Jesus would want to return to Judea where his life is at risk (v 8). They also misunderstand Jesus' reference to Lazarus sleeping (v 12), and Thomas seems to get completely the wrong end of the stick (v 16).

Confusion reigns! But then it often does at moments of pain, uncertainty and challenge. We can find it hard to see how God is at work at such times. How we respond to this lack of clarity is a significant test of our faith and our trust in Jesus.

> 'This illness will not end in death. No, it is for God's glory so that God's Son may be glorified through it.'
>
> **John 11:4**

RESPOND

Is there a situation in your life where it seems confusion reigns? Express your trust in Jesus today, even despite the lack of clarity.

Bible in a year: Isaiah 15,16; Psalm 103

Tuesday 10 September
John 11:17–27

A light in the fog

PREPARE
How would you have responded to Jesus' 'delay' in visiting Lazarus?

. . . .

READ
John 11:17–27

EXPLORE
Have you ever woken up one morning and been greeted with blanket fog? Fog can be beautiful but also troubling. Driving in thick fog can be disconcerting, for example, even dangerous. Yesterday we saw the 'fog' of the confused disciples. They were bemused by Jesus' actions and words. Why delay visiting Lazarus? Why the talk of falling asleep? Today we are introduced to Lazarus' sister Martha who is also living in the fog of the same troubling and painful situation.

Martha rushes out to meet Jesus as he nears her home and immediately confronts him: 'if you had been here, my brother would not have died' (v 21). She is in a deeply painful moment with the death of her brother and Jesus' seeming indifference. She expresses herself and yet this expression of pain is accompanied by a deep declaration of trust in Jesus: 'But I know that even now God will give you whatever you ask' (v 22). Like a bright torch piercing through the fog, Martha offers a light of trust through the mist of uncertainty.

Martha's example of faith is a profound and moving one to us. She openly and honestly expresses her frustration and confusion, yet also her overriding trust in the goodness and sovereignty of God.

> 'But I know that even now God will give you whatever you ask.'
>
> **John 11:22**

RESPOND
Trusting Jesus in painful, confusing or frustrating circumstances can be one of the greatest challenges to our faith. Whatever situation you find yourself in today, follow the example of Martha who expresses trust amid uncertainty.

. . . .

Bible in a year: Isaiah 17–20; Titus 1

God's mysterious ways

PREPARE

What comfort might you take from this short verse in today's reading: 'Jesus wept' (v 35)?

READ

John 11:28–44

EXPLORE

In 1773, English poet and hymnwriter William Cowper wrote the hymn 'God Moves in a Mysterious Way'. It proved a popular hymn but also gave to the English language an enduring expression we still use today. God's ways of sovereignly working in our lives can often seem deeply mysterious. Today we arrive at the culmination of the Lazarus story, and we read the extraordinary words 'The dead man came out' (v 44). Dead men do not 'come out'; they do not speak or walk or live or breathe. And yet that is what we see here. What a mystery!

At this stage in the story, John shows us Mary, who expresses confusion as well as doubt and pain. While Jesus doesn't share her confusion or doubt, he does share her pain. The shortest verse in the Bible profoundly points to the pain felt by Jesus at this moment of deep sorrow for Martha and Mary: 'Jesus wept' (v 35).

These two simple words can be of huge comfort to us. God may indeed move in mysterious ways. He is, however, not indifferent to our pain and our situations. The wonder of the incarnation of Jesus – God entering into humanity and becoming human – tells us that God is neither indifferent nor distant. In the mystery of our pain and our lives, God is present.

Jesus wept.

John 11:35

RESPOND

Take time to thank Jesus for his presence in your life in all circumstances.

Bible in a year: Isaiah 21,22; Titus 2

Thursday 12 September
John 11:45–57

An unlikely partnership

PREPARE

What has been the most important meeting you've ever been involved in?

READ

John 11:45–57

EXPLORE

The first time a man meets his future wife. A job interview for a dream job. The emergency board meeting to discuss closing the company. Some meetings are more consequential than others. Today we read of an important gathering between the Pharisees and the chief priests which changed the course of history. These two groups had deeply different outlooks on how Jewish life should be lived out. However, a mutual dislike of Jesus leads these two parties to become unlikely partners. The raising of Lazarus – a very public act of extraordinary supernatural power – proves a catalyst for their partnership: 'So from that day on they plotted to take his life' (v 53).

What causes these two groups to work together? Surely jealousy of Jesus' popularity plays a part as they could see the crowds flocking to Jesus. Jealousy, but also fear. They were deeply afraid of their future and their security: 'the Romans will come and take away both our temple and our nation' (v 48). Following Jesus should lead us not to fear our future, but rather to have deep satisfaction in where we are heading – both ultimately but also in this life. A life lived close to Jesus, listening to his voice and following his commands, is the best way to live.

> So from that day on they plotted to take his life.
>
> **John 11:53**

RESPOND

Ask Jesus, the one who never doubted the future of Lazarus, to help you live a life of peace and contentment in your present and for your future.

Bible in a year: Isaiah 23,24; Titus 3

Waste not, want not!

PREPARE:

How do you think you would have responded to Mary's extravagant, 'wasteful' act described in these verses?

• •

READ

John 12:1–11

EXPLORE

We are programmed by our culture and those around us not to waste a thing – whether it's food, water, energy, time or money. We can be aghast if someone throws away perfectly good food, or feel let down by someone who doesn't use their God-given talents to their full potential. 'What a waste!' we cry!

Today we read of a 'waste' of 'expensive perfume' (v 3) which is accompanied by the reaction of the scandalised Judas. John tells us how Mary lavishly pours this perfume on Jesus resulting in the house being 'filled with the fragrance of the perfume' (v 3). Jesus quickly rebukes and corrects Judas (vs 7,8). This is no waste but rather a beautiful act of love and devotion. As the Jewish authorities step up their plot to kill not only Jesus but also Lazarus (v 10), Mary's actions are the opposite – a generous act of worship to Jesus who will soon be leaving them.

The challenge for us as followers of Jesus is to follow the example of Mary and not that of Judas or the religious leaders. We're called to live lives of extravagant devotion to Jesus where we give our best, not looking around us or counting the cost.

> Then Mary took about half a litre of ... expensive perfume; she poured it on Jesus' feet and wiped his feet with her hair. And the house was filled with the fragrance of the perfume.
>
> **John 12:3**

RESPOND

Ask God to show you specific ways in which you can show your own lavish and generous devotion to him.

• •

Bible in a year: Isaiah 25,26; Psalm 104

Saturday 14 September
John 12:12–19

An arrival like no other

PREPARE
As you read this familiar story of Jesus entering Jerusalem on a donkey, ask God to speak to you afresh.

READ
John 12:12–19

EXPLORE
Although the narrative of the raising of Lazarus is over, John shows us how it continues to have a ripple effect, inspiring some (vs 17,18) and infuriating others (v 19). The nature of that miracle has both similarities and differences to the event we read of today – the triumphal entry of Jesus into Jerusalem. Both events are public, attracting large crowds and strong reactions. Both have Jesus at the centre of the action, and both reveal aspects of who Jesus is.

Yet while the raising of Lazarus shows Jesus' power, the arrival into Jerusalem shows us his humility. He comes into the great city of David not riding on a horse or lifted high on a carriage, but sat on the back of a 'young donkey' (vs 14,15). The great King of kings, the incarnate Son of God rides humbly on a donkey. This is the kingship of Jesus in one simple image.

John is slowly revealing to us who Jesus is. He's one who, yes, heals the blind and raises the dead, but he is also one who weeps with the grieving and rides on donkeys. What a God we serve and follow! Strength and simplicity; power and humility.

> They took palm branches and went out to meet him, shouting, 'Hosanna!' 'Blessed is he who comes in the name of the Lord!' 'Blessed is the king of Israel!'
> **John 12:13**

RESPOND
Take time to worship and thank Jesus for his profound humility. Ask him to show you areas of your life where humility has not yet taken root.

Peaceful sleep

PREPARE
Do you regularly get a good night's sleep? Allow today's psalm to speak to your heart.

READ
Psalm 4

EXPLORE
Bad sleep affects many of us. Getting to sleep can be difficult; unpleasant dreams or the worries of the day can lead to wakefulness. David ends Psalm 4 with a simple declaration: 'In peace I will lie down and sleep' (v 8). Despite his many dramatic trials which would cause most of us to have sleepless nights, David claims to sleep in peace.

The secret to his peaceful nights lies in his conviction that the God of the universe hears him and answers him. David's God is a personal one. When one reflects on this truth, the repercussions are enormous. The great King of the universe hears us when we call to him (see v 3) and takes an interest in our lives. If we hold to this conviction, it becomes natural to follow David's next step and 'trust in the LORD' (v 5).

A path to a life lived in peace starts with the simple, almost childlike conviction that God cares for me; like a good father he has my best interests at heart. And if this is the case, I can live my life in abounding trust in him which, in turn, leads to a peaceful life; both during the day and the night.

In peace I will lie down and sleep, for you alone, LORD, make me dwell in safety.

Psalm 4:8

RESPOND
Do you live a life of peace or chaos? Trust or anxiety? Ask God to help you see his deep personal care of you and enter into a life of peace.

Bible in a year: Isaiah 29,30; Hebrews 1

Ordinary family, extraordinary future

I love learning from the giants of scripture – for example, Abraham, Moses, David, Elijah or Peter, John and Paul – but their lives can sometimes seem out of reach and out of touch with ours. This story of Ruth is about an ordinary family, living in a traumatic time of injustice and violence, where Israel has once again turned away from God. It is a beautiful story of the faith and friendship of two women and God's faithful provision for them.

About the writer
Erica Roberts

Married with three adult children, Erica enjoys walking, cold water swimming and reading. She loves her role as City Chaplain for Older People in Southampton, and learning from the wisdom of those God has called her to serve.

As I write this, refugees seeking asylum are in the news again, fleeing from famine, war and injustice. We can almost hear the story of Naomi and Elimelek in our media today. Tragedy ensues, and Naomi's raw experience of loss and bereavement will resonate with many of us. Despite the traumatic beginning, as the story unfolds we get caught up in the narrative of God's redemptive purposes for this family.

The story also looks ahead as we witness God's covenantal promise to Abraham, 'all peoples on earth will be blessed through you' (Genesis 12:3), take root in the marriage between Boaz and Ruth, a Moabite woman, both refugee and Gentile, who, as our story concludes, gives birth to a son who begins the lineage through King David to the King of all kings, our Sovereign Lord Jesus.

Here is an extraordinary story about God's loving kindness to an ordinary family.

Discerning God's way

PREPARE

Reflect on how God has shown you the way ahead. 'Stand at the crossroads and look; ask for the ancient paths, ask where the good way is, and walk in it' (Jeremiah 6:16).

. . . .

READ

Ruth 1:1–18

EXPLORE

Life is full of choices. Each day we make choices of little consequence, but occasionally we are required to grapple with tough, life-changing decisions, affecting both ourselves and those around us.

We find our protagonists at crossroads today, each required to make a life-changing choice. We know little about Elimelek's decision to leave Bethlehem for Moab, except that he heads to a pagan country which has oppressed Israel for years (Judges 3:12–14). Elimelek wants to provide for his family, but I wonder about the motivation behind his decision-making.

Despite overwhelming grief, Naomi responds to a faithful God, who has now intervened in the famine (v 6). Accompanied by her daughters-in-law, Naomi finds the courage to return home. Blessing Orpah and Ruth, she entreats them to return to Moab and rebuild

their lives. After impassioned persuasion, Orpah agrees, but Ruth responds with indignation, committing her life to serve both Naomi and the God of Israel (v17). In making her decision, Ruth is drawn to Naomi's relationship with a personal and compassionate God. Capturing this hope, Ruth makes a life-changing choice that places her in history. I wonder if we, like Ruth, are drawn towards God's path for our life when making decisions.

'... Where you go I will go, and where you stay I will stay. Your people will be my people and your God my God.'

Ruth 1:16

RESPOND

'Show me your ways, Lord, teach me your paths' (Psalm 25:4). Invite God to show you his ways as you make choices today.

. . . .

Bible in a year: Isaiah 31,32; Psalm 105

Tuesday 17 September
Ruth 1:19 – 2:13

A marketplace

PREPARE

Consider a time when you have been aware of God's provision in your life. Praise God for his abundant generosity.

READ
Ruth 1:19 – 2:13

EXPLORE

'It's my lifeline. I couldn't survive without it.' This is one mother's response to a social enterprise project in Southampton. Called Marketplace,* this charity provides an empowering addition to the established food banks. For a weekly £5 membership, each family not only selects quality food provisions, but becomes part of a welcoming and supportive community aimed at improving health and well-being.

God's compassion for the poor, the oppressed and the foreigner is expressed through socio-economic laws reflecting his concern for the vulnerable. In Deuteronomy we read that God 'defends the cause of the fatherless and the widow, and loves the foreigner residing among you, giving them food and clothing' (Deuteronomy 10:18). Levitical law required edges of fields to remain unharvested, not to collect fallen grain and never to strip vineyards bare, therefore providing for 'the poor and for the foreigner' (Leviticus 23:22).

*https://southamptoncitymission.co.uk/marketplace

Returning to our story today, Ruth, a poor widow and a foreigner, is found gleaning behind the harvesters (v 3). We discover that, by God's grace, this field belongs to Boaz, a relative of Naomi's husband, Elimelek. Boaz, reflecting God's generosity and recognising Ruth's faithful companionship to Naomi (v 12), offers further provision through female friendship, protection and refreshment (v 9). What a wonderful example of an ancient 'Marketplace'.

'May the LORD repay you for what you have done. May you be richly rewarded by the LORD, the God of Israel ...'
Ruth 2:12

RESPOND

Pray: 'Loving Father, show me how I can both be a voice for the voiceless and offer practical help. Amen.'

Bible in a year: Isaiah 33,34; Hebrews 2

Lovingkindness

PREPARE

Reflect on these words: 'The LORD's lovingkindnesses indeed never cease, For His compassions never fail. *They* are new every morning; Great is Your faithfulness' (Lamentations 3:22,23, NASB1995).

READ

Ruth 2:14–23

EXPLORE

I wonder if you've tried learning a new language. I've loved grappling with some basic French over this past year. It's interesting to work out how new phrases might be used, but I remain bewildered at those words that just can't be translated directly into English.

In the book of Ruth, a similar translation issue arises with the wonderful Hebrew word, *hesed*, used on three occasions as Naomi blesses her daughters-in-law (1:8), when Naomi speaks of Boaz (2:20) and finally when Boaz recognises the generosity of Ruth (3:10). The roots of *hesed* lie in God's covenant relationship with his people, referring to God's unconditional love and unending loyalty. *Hesed*, translated here as kindness, runs deeper than a simple emotion, but is reflected in God's compassionate mercy, which remains unbroken despite the brokenness of humanity.

Naomi understands the gracious, kindness bestowed by Boaz on Ruth (v 20). We begin to see how God's restoration for these two widows unfolds through this beautiful story, a restoration that gives us a foretaste of God's *hesed* for humanity, in all its brokenness, ultimately expressed by God's forgiveness for our sin, through the sacrificial love of his Son, Jesus Christ.

'The LORD bless him!' Naomi said to her daughter-in-law. 'He has not stopped showing his kindness to the living and the dead.'

Ruth 2:20

RESPOND

Praise God for his lovingkindness and his unending grace.

Bible in a year: Isaiah 35,36; Hebrews 3

Thursday 19 September
Ruth 3:1–18

Under his wings

PREPARE

'He will cover you with his feathers, and under his wings you will find refuge' (Psalm 91:4). Enjoy imagining how it feels to rest under God's protective wings.

READ
Ruth 3:1–18

EXPLORE

Proposals of marriage today are becoming increasingly elaborate, from treasure hunts, to prearranged public declarations, or even taking to the ocean in a kayak – all provide modern settings to pop the question. In the climax of our story, Naomi manoeuvres Ruth into a position for a proposal of marriage to Boaz: a vulnerable, bold and yet strategic move to ensure Ruth's future security (v 1).

Although unorthodox, the wider context is that Boaz was the kinsman-redeemer (v 9), responsible to safeguard the family, including marrying the childless widow to perpetuate the family name, as stated in levirate law (Deuteronomy 25:5–10). Although creeping through the dark to lie at Boaz's feet may seem provocative, culturally it was viewed as an act of submission. Trusting Boaz, whom she'd come to respect, Ruth approached Boaz humbly and courageously, to be redeemed in marriage.

'Spreading the corner of your garment' (v 9), sometimes translated as 'wing', was an ancient custom, where kinsmen claimed a widow in marriage. Boaz had already prayed God's protection over Ruth, 'under whose wings you have come to take refuge' (2:12). Covering Ruth in this way, providing protection and security through marriage, reminds us of God's commitment to cover us under his loving, protective care.

… 'Spread the corner of your garment over me, since you are a guardian-redeemer of our family.'

Ruth 3:9

RESPOND
Pray for someone who needs to shelter under God's protective wings today.

Bible in a year: Isaiah 37,38; Hebrews 4

Public witness

PREPARE
Meditate on these lyrics: 'There is a redeemer, / Jesus, God's own Son, / Precious Lamb of God, Messiah / Holy One.'*

READ
Ruth 4:1–12

EXPLORE
Over the years, we have all attended wedding ceremonies. I love the moments that involve those supporting the wedding couple: 'We will,' declared fervently by family and friends. And that sacred moment in the Anglican service, when the stole is wrapped around the couple's hands: 'Therefore what God has joined together, let no one separate' (Mark 10:9). An integral part of the covenant-making in marriage is public witness, an accountability to the wider community, recognising both their ongoing support for the couple and their prayers.

In our story today, uncertainty hangs in the air as Boaz rushes to the city gate, where elders gathered, and judicial matters were resolved. Boaz has transactions to make, and they have to be witnessed in public. We discover there is another kinsman-redeemer closer in line than Boaz (vs 3,4). Boaz strategically manoeuvres the discussion so the unnamed kinsman realises the personal sacrifice of marrying Ruth, a Moabite (v 6). This first transaction is witnessed with the traditional transfer of a shoe (v 7); Boaz can now officially redeem Ruth in marriage. This is done publicly in front of the elders, receiving not only their public acknowledgement of this union, but also their blessing for Boaz and Ruth's life together (vs 11,12).

'I have also acquired Ruth the Moabite, Mahlon's widow, as my wife ... Today you are witnesses!'

Ruth 4:10

RESPOND
Pray: 'Loving Father, help me to support and pray for married couples I am privileged to know and love. Amen.'

*'There is a Redeemer', Melody Green, Capitol Christian Music Group, 1982

Bible in a year: Isaiah 39,40; Psalm 106

Being connected

PREPARE

'I will be a Father to you, and you will be my sons and daughters, says the Lord Almighty' (2 Corinthians 6:18). Give thanks as we celebrate our place in God's family.

READ

Ruth 4:13–22

EXPLORE

I love being connected to a network of family and friends. I wonder whether you've done your family history, rooting and connecting you back in time. I have a Scottish heritage. My father's family, the 'Mackies', were dairy farmers from Aberdeenshire, and it brings a smile as I place a tub of Mackie's ice cream in my shopping trolley!

Our story returns to Naomi, as she rejoices at the blessing of being placed in a new family for her older years. We can see God's sovereignty in how life has unfolded through tragedy, bereavement and loss. Throughout, Naomi has placed her hope in a faithful God and, centuries later, Paul, writing to the church in Rome, pays tribute to this same God when he says, 'in all things God works for the good of those who love him' (Romans 8:28).

Our connectedness also looks ahead, whether through children and grandchildren, or perhaps a sense of our care for God's world for future generations. In Ruth, we have seen signs of God's redemptive purpose and as the story closes we understand that, looking ahead, through the gift of her child, comes the lineage connecting directly to Jesus, both our kinsman and our redeemer for all of humanity (vs 17,22).

> And they named him Obed. He was the father of Jesse, the father of David.
>
> **Ruth 4:17**

RESPOND

Pray: 'Sovereign Lord Jesus, strengthen our faith, so we can trust that in all things you are working for our good. Amen.'

Bible in a year: Isaiah 41,42; Hebrews 5

Waiting expectantly...

PREPARE

'Do not be anxious about anything, but in every situation, by prayer and petition, with thanksgiving, present your requests to God' (Philippians 4:6). Offer God your deepest cares and concerns.

READ

Psalm 5

EXPLORE

I suspect we have all cried out to God in desperation, maybe even with those words, 'Are you really there, God?' I can still feel the raw grief years later, when after several miscarriages I stood on an empty beach in the middle of winter, screaming at God across the waves and into the wind. I didn't doubt his presence, I hadn't stopped trusting him, but I was angry and confused. Like the psalmist (vs 1,2), there was an urgency in the prayer, a lament for my situation and a cry for help.

The psalmist's cry arises from a life of persistent and expectant prayer. Approaching God each morning, the psalmist both lays his requests before God, and 'waits expectantly' for God to respond (v 3). Prayer is integral to the psalmist's relationship with a faithful God, so that when crises arrive, the place of refuge where honest emotions can be revealed is in that place of prayer, in communion with a compassionate God.

The evangelist Billy Graham once said: 'True prayer is a way of life, not just for use in cases of emergency. Make it a habit, and when the need arises you will be in practice.'

In the morning, LORD, you hear my voice; in the morning I lay my requests before you and wait expectantly.

Psalm 5:3

RESPOND

Ask God to show you how you could refresh and reinvigorate your prayer life this coming week.

Bible in a year: Isaiah 43,44; Hebrews 6

Joy amid opposition

Philippi was a mixed place. It was a Roman colony, which meant that Roman law ruled in the city. A sprinkling of Roman army veterans had plots of land, among a majority of native Greeks. Perhaps a quarter of the population were Roman citizens. The city had many temples, including for the worship of the emperor, which presented a challenge to people who worshipped Jesus as Lord (Philippians 2:9–11).

About the writer
Steve Walton

Steve Walton is Senior Research Fellow in New Testament of Trinity College, Bristol. He has taught in colleges and universities in Bedford, Cambridge, London and Nottingham. He is a retired international volleyball referee, and lives with his wife, Ali, and their Border Terrier, Flora.

Paul, Timothy and Silas planted the church there after a vision (Acts 16:9). After initial success in Lydia's conversion (Acts 16:13–15), Paul clashed with the owners of a fortune-telling slave girl after he delivered her from a spirit (Acts 16:16–21). Paul and Silas were freed from prison after a series of incidents and left a small group of believers based in Lydia's home (Acts 16:40).

The Philippian believers had sent financial support to Paul more than once, most recently through Epaphroditus (Philippians 2:25–30; 4:18), and this letter is in part expressing Paul's thanks (4:10,14–19). It is also one of Paul's warmest letters, full of the theme of joy (1:4,18,25; 2:2,17,18,29; 3:1; 4:1,4,10) – this despite the evidence that the believers faced opposition from both Jews and Gentiles (1:27–30; 3:2,18,19).

Why not read the letter through at a sitting to get an overall impression before you dive into the detail? It should take 15–20 minutes.

Why be thankful?

PREPARE

Think of people who have helped you to begin and grow in your Christian faith. Spend a few minutes giving thanks to God for them.

READ

Philippians 1:1–6

EXPLORE

In his letter to the Philippians, Paul expresses great affection for his readers. Greek letters conventionally begin with a thanksgiving for the recipient, and Paul expands and Christianises this standard opening. Paul's is not just human warmth, as towards a good friend. This is thankfulness to God for the results of his work among the believers (v 6). Paul thanks God regularly for them and rejoices for two key reasons.

First, they share in Paul's gospel ministry as he travels around the Greek and Roman world planting and establishing new churches (v 5). This certainly includes their praying for his work (1:19), and they also support him financially (4:14–18). Their money frees Paul from having to work to support himself, as he did in Corinth until Timothy brought the Philippians' gift for him (Acts 18:1–5).

Secondly, Paul is confident that God will finish the work he has started in the Philippians' lives (v 6). The God Paul serves does not do half measures: when God starts a job, he carries through to completion. Paul looks forward with anticipation and confidence to 'the day of Christ Jesus', when Jesus returns to earth and finally and fully transforms believers to be the people he wants them to be (see 3:20,21).

I thank my God every time I remember you.

Philippians 1:3

RESPOND

Return to thanksgiving to God, focusing now on the confident hope we have in God completing our transformation to be like Jesus.

Bible in a year: Isaiah 45,46; Psalm 107

Tuesday 24 September
Philippians 1:7–11

Praying with Paul

PREPARE

Who are the people who 'share in God's grace' with you (v 7)? Give thanks for their partnership with you in the Christian life of grace and gospel service.

READ
Philippians 1:7–11

EXPLORE

When Paul prays, he prays strategically. He focuses on believers' spiritual growth, rather than bodily illnesses or socio-economic circumstances. His first concern is how they live in their situation. He longs for them to know God better and love God more with heart, soul, mind and strength (Mark 12:30). He asks for a growing love (v 9), which – like everything he prays for – comes through Jesus (v 11). This is not mere emotion: it overflows in understanding, which enables them to recognise the right way to live and to carry it out (vs 9,10).

The combination of love and knowledge is vital. Without love – for God and people – we are shadows of God's purposes for us. Love without discernment produces ethical relativism which leaves us as we are, rather than being transformed to be 'pure and blameless' (v 10). God's love is like that: God loves us as we are, but not to stay as we are, for he has better things in store!

Paul doesn't just pray these things: he tells his hearers (they heard the letter read aloud) that he is praying for them. There's power in telling people what we are praying for them – then they can look expectantly to God for these things.

And this is my prayer: that your love may abound more and more in knowledge and depth of insight.

Philippians 1:9

RESPOND
Pray verses 9–11 over the next few days for those you thought of earlier and let them know that you're praying in this way.

Bible in a year: Isaiah 47,48; Hebrews 7

In chains for Christ

PREPARE
Imagine being in prison with Paul. How would you feel? What fears would you have?

. . . .

READ
Philippians 1:12–26

EXPLORE
It was grim being in a Roman prison: inmates needed friends to bring food and warm clothes, since none were supplied. They could stay there for years if they weren't high enough up the social pecking order. Paul's hearers were concerned about both Paul's well-being and the repercussions of his being imprisoned for the gospel.

First, Paul makes clear that he continues to speak the gospel among the Roman guard (v 13), and his courageous testimony has encouraged other believers to do the same (v 14). His top priority is that people hear of Christ and respond to him (v 18). His Christian testimony is enhanced, not damaged, through imprisonment.

Secondly, he expresses confidence that he will continue to be faithful to Christ as they pray for him, and as the Spirit enables him (v 19). Indeed, he rejoices, even in prison, because of these things

(vs 18,19). He looks death in the face with hope, for on its other side he will meet Christ (v 23), even though he believes he will keep working for Christ on earth (vs 22,25).

So the Philippians need not fear on Paul's account: he is right at the centre of God's purposes for him and expects to see them again (v 25). Through Paul they will grow and rejoice.

> … I know that through your prayers and God's provision of the Spirit of Jesus Christ what has happened to me will turn out for my deliverance.
>
> **Philippians 1:19**

RESPOND
Pray for Christians who suffer for their faith today, that they will be faithful to Christ and know his joy.

. . . .

Bible in a year: Isaiah 49,50; Hebrews 8

Stand united in suffering

PREPARE

Consider how you have lived in a manner not worthy of the gospel in the past few days. Confess these failures and ask God's forgiveness through Jesus.

READ

Philippians 1:27–30

EXPLORE

'Conduct yourselves' (v 27) means 'live as citizens', that is, live in the public square among your fellow citizens (the related noun, 'citizenship', is used in 3:20). Their faith in Jesus is not a private affair but must influence and transform their lives in Philippi. This would be challenging, for they would have to refuse or resist aspects of Philippian life, such as joining in festivals to other gods. Others might misunderstand or be actively hostile, and they might suffer (v 29).

Imagine a couple who are bakers in Philippi who become Christians. What would change? They would remove the statue of the city's patron god from the counter in their shop, resulting in customers suspecting disloyalty to the city, and their sales would drop. Fellow bakers would refuse help when they had a big order and needed to borrow other ovens. Their suffering would be economic. They might lose their business and have to beg.

In that situation, other believers' support would be critical: to 'stand firm in the one Spirit' (v 27) would include both prayer and practical help. These Christian bakers would need other believers to buy their bread. This support, enabled by the Spirit, would enable them not to be frightened (v 28).

For it has been granted to you on behalf of Christ not only to believe in him, but also to suffer for him.

Philippians 1:29

RESPOND

Think of Christians known to you who suffer. Are there prayerful and practical ways in which you can support them? Act on this!

Life together

PREPARE
Give thanks for the unity you see in your church and ask God to give more of it.

READ
Philippians 2:1–4

EXPLORE
Paul bombards his hearers with unity language: 'like-minded', 'the same love', 'one in spirit and of one mind' (v 2). In a time when believers are opposed (1:28–30), mutual support is vital. Paul calls them to hold together through all God does for and in them, making a list of what God gives them (v 1). It is not, then, that the Philippians must screw themselves up to put up with each other: their unity flows from God's love and generosity to them.

At the centre of unity is humility (v 3). In the ancient world, humility is not a virtue: the philosopher Epictetus wrote: 'Who wishes to live ... humbly? No one.' The word is given a completely different connotation by the life, teaching, and humiliating death of Jesus (see 2:8), for Jesus valued others at a cost, to the extent of dying for us. Paul contrasts humility with 'selfish ambition'. Competitive self-promotion is normal in the Roman Empire, seeking honour or power or wealth, and looking down on those who don't have these things. Instead, humility is about other-regard (v 3), about acting to benefit others (v 4) – having a mindset which values others and being ready to support and enable them to live for Christ.

> ... not looking to your own interests but each of you to the interests of the others.
>
> **Philippians 2:4**

RESPOND
Reflect on how you might value others above yourself in your church, workplace or home. What specific step(s) can you take to demonstrate this? Pray about how and when to act.

Bible in a year: Isaiah 53,54; Psalms 108,109

Glory through humiliation

PREPARE

Draw a parabola. Write 'in very nature God' (v 6) at the top left, and 'Jesus Christ is Lord' (v 11) at the top right. Trace Jesus' journey by writing key phrases down and up the parabola.

READ
Philippians 2:5–11

EXPLORE

Paul becomes lyrical in expounding Jesus' journey from glory back to glory via becoming human and dying in humiliation. There were popular stories of gods coming to earth in Paul's world, but those gods did not give up their powers or status – they could angrily hurt or kill people. Their human appearance was a temporary cloak. Not so Jesus: Paul parallels Jesus being 'in very nature God' (v 6) with taking 'the very nature of a servant' (v 7) in becoming human. Rather than powerfully 'zapping' people, he served his Father humbly and obediently all the way to a humiliating death on a cross (v 8).

This wonderful self-giving is why Jesus is now exalted above everything and everyone (v 9). Paul echoes Isaiah 45:23, a passage about God's rule, and puts Jesus at its heart: Jesus is now recognised as Lord of all (vs 10,11), greater than rulers such as Caesar. As often in the New Testament, Paul picks up a scriptural passage about God and treats Jesus as its subject, showing that Jesus is the one true God become one of us.

'By myself I have sworn, my mouth has uttered in all integrity a word that will not be revoked: before me every knee will bow; by me every tongue will swear.'

Isaiah 45:23

RESPOND

Praise God for Jesus' willingness to travel this journey for our sake, and worship him as Lord. Notice verse 5. What does it mean for your life to have this 'mindset'?

Bible in a year: Isaiah 55,56; Hebrews 10

Penitence and assurance

PREPARE
Reflect on ways you are failing to be the person God calls you to be. Spend time confessing these sins to God and asking forgiveness.

READ
Psalm 6

EXPLORE

This psalm combines pain and confidence remarkably. The writer brings their despair and anguish to God (vs 1–7). The Lord is the source of the suffering, for the psalmist appeals for freedom from God's deserved rebuke and discipline (v 1). These verses portray how to speak to God when we suffer, especially when it is because of our sin. Notice the graphic images (vs 5–7).

Amid pain, the writer appeals for God's help (vs 2–4). It's all too easy when we suffer, especially when we suffer because of our sins, to dwell on our pain and fail to look to God. This psalm encourages us to take our pain to God honestly, to confess our failure, and to ask for restoration.

The change in verses 8–10 is amazing! Something has brought renewed confidence, perhaps an encouraging word from another or the realisation that God will hear. This part of the psalm sits between being assured that God will answer and the arrival of that answer. Praying this way makes a difference not because it changes the psalmist but, much more importantly, because of the assurance of God's response. God hears and will act.

The LORD has heard my cry for mercy; the LORD accepts my prayer.
Psalm 6:9

RESPOND
Think of a time you were struggling in your life. How did you respond? Does this psalm offer you a different way of dealing with such situations for the future? Talk with God about that.

Bible in a year: Isaiah 57,58; Hebrews 11

Monday 30 September
Philippians 2:12–18

We work... God works

PREPARE

What has changed in your life because you follow Jesus? Reflect on this and give thanks to God for how he is changing you to be like Jesus.

READ

Philippians 2:12–18

EXPLORE

Paul builds on the model of Jesus (vs 6–11), drawing implications for his hearers: 'Therefore' (v 12). As Jesus obeyed his Father, believers are called to obey, for that it is where God's power and blessing come. They aren't doing this to earn their salvation, in the sense of belonging to Christ now and at the judgement day – but they are *working out* their salvation. They are walking on the Christian path, and aren't alone, for as they walk in obedience to God, God does two remarkable things (v 13). He both directs their wills in his paths and gives them power to act in tune with his purposes.

After such amazing words, we come to earth with a bump in Paul's call not to grumble or argue (v 14). This is where the rubber hits the road. Paul has the grumpy Israelites in the wilderness in mind, echoing Deuteronomy 32:5 (v 15). Churches can be, and are, split by negative speech – words can do enormous damage to others. The tongue is like a fire which can burn down a forest (James 3:5,6), but Christian speech is to shine with the light of God's Word (vs 15,16).

> ... for it is God who works in you to will and to act in order to fulfil his good purpose.
>
> **Philippians 2:13**

RESPOND

Audit your speech over the past 24 hours: give thanks where it shines with God's Word and ask God's forgiveness (and maybe other people's too) where you have grumbled or argued.

Bible in a year: Isaiah 59,60; Psalms 110,111